God Knew

Faithfulness Fulfilled

A Story of Love & God's Promise

James W. and Linda M. Meyer

TITLETOWN
PUBLISHING

TitleTown Publishing, LLC
P.O. Box 12093 Green Bay, WI 54307-12093
920.737.8051 | titletownpublishing.com
Publisher: Tracy C. Ertl

Designer: Erika L. Block
Editor: Lori A. Preuss

Engagement photography courtesy of Craig Stodola
Craig John Photography | craigjohn.com

Wedding Photography courtesy of Christy Janeczko
Christy Janeczko Photography | christyjphotography.com

PUBLISHER'S CATALOGING-IN-PUBLICATION DATA:

Prepared by Cassidy Cataloguing Services, Inc.

Names: Meyer, James W., author. | Meyer, Linda M., 1963- author.

Title: Faithfulness fulfilled: a story of love & God's promise / James W. and Linda M. Meyer.

Description: Green Bay, WI : TitleTown Publishing, [2023] | Series: God knew. | Includes bibliographical references.

Identifiers: ISBN: 978-1-955047-24-1 (trade paper) | 978-1-955047-25-8 (ebook)

Subjects: LCSH: Christian biography. | Christian life. | Faith (Christianity) | Spiritual life--Christianity. | God (Christianity)--Love. | God (Christianity)--Promises. | God (Christianity)--Knowableness. | God (Christianity)--Omniscience. | LCGFT: Auto-biographies. | BISAC: RELIGION / Christian Living / Family & Relationships. | RELIGION / Christian Living / Personal Memoirs.

Classification: LCC: BR1700.3 .M49 2023 | DDC: 248.4--dc23

DEDICATION

We dedicate this book to:

God, our Heavenly Father, Who out of His great love for us, sent His only begotten Son, Jesus Christ, to live a perfect life, and to die on the cross for our sins, that whoever believes in Him will not perish, but have eternal life. This is the greatest act of love the world has ever known. We are also thankful for the Holy Spirit working faith in our hearts to believe in Jesus as our Savior, and for sustaining that faith each day.

Our parents, Ralph and Lorraine Meyer, and Richard and Fritzi Leighton. Thank you for always loving us and for being powerful role models in our lives. We love you and we miss you very much. And we look forward with certain hope to that joyous reunion in heaven.

Special thanks to our moms for always praying for us to find a Christian spouse to spend our "happily ever after" with. Your prayers have been answered.

ACKNOWLEDGEMENTS

Linda's Acknowledgements

To Pastor Jerry and Sherry Brooks, you have always modeled to me what it means to walk the walk and talk the talk of the Christian life. For most of my life, I have seen you as my second parents and I love you both dearly. Your preaching and teaching have always been spot-on biblically, and your wise leadership and mentoring made me want to walk out my faith with reverence for God and always giving Him the glory for all my blessings. Forty-three years is a long time to share friendship and ministry, and I know God still has much more work for us all to do for His Kingdom. As you often say, "The BEST is yet to come!"

To Jeff and Tammi Ratliff, you are more like brother and sister to me, in addition to being the best of friends. You both have been there for me through thick and thin and have spoken so much life and encouragement to me. You walked through many trials with losing my brother (and your friend), and then both of my parents, and I have done the same for you. Jeff, you tell the best stories one minute, and then you speak strong words of wisdom the next. Tammi, you have been my best friend for so long. I love that all we have to do is look at each other and we know exactly what the other is thinking. We definitely epitomize that meme that says, "if it's a don't laugh situation, don't look over at me." I treasure our friendship and love the memories we have made over the years and all the laughter we have shared. Thank you both for being so weird and awesome and for being our matron-of-honor. I love you, Buddy.

To the leadership and my friends at Proverbs 31 Ministries, thank you for believing in me and trusting me to be a ministry volunteer for the many years that I did so. Thank you for being my "online friends" during some of the hardest days I have walked through. Lysa TerKeurst, you will never know how much the wisdom and encouragement of your writing and your ministry leadership shaped me into the woman I am today. Melissa Taylor, thank you for your friendship and for listening to

God and stepping out in faith to start a "little online Bible study" that now speaks into the lives of hundreds of thousands of people throughout the world each year. You are an amazing group of women who love the Lord with everything in you and your vision to eliminate biblical poverty for women all over the world is life-changing. You also bring direction, mentorship, and opportunity for women who want to write or speak through your yearly "She Speaks" program. The things I learned through that program helped me to have the courage to step out in faith and sit down at a computer and write the words of this book. The impact you are making in people's lives is priceless, and I was honored to be part of it.

To my family, we are a bit spread out now, but I am so thankful for parents that taught us how to be not just siblings but to be friends. Our lives have taken a major turn in the last year after losing Dad, but I am so thankful that we had the extra time together last year to help each other get through his loss and the loss of our "normal." I love you all so much. Let's keep Mom and Dad's legacy alive—it's up to us now!

To my loving husband, Jim. God truly knew what he was doing when He directed our roads to meet. He answered my "but God you promised" prayer in the most amazing way and our God-honoring story is one for the ages. Thank you for being my earthly rock, my confidante, bringing me more laughter than I could have ever imagined, and for loving me with all the love in your heart. I love you, Mine. Forever and always!

Jim's Acknowledgements

To Pastor Timothy Shoup, you are my pastor, but you are also my mentor, my confidante, my sounding board, one of my best friends, and our best man. Thank you for always providing me with the Godly perspective I need to face any situation, and for nurturing my faith. We are blessed to have you in our lives.

To my beautiful and amazing wife, Linda. You are the long-awaited answer to many prayers, and God knew exactly the woman I would need. Thank you for always loving me and for supporting my dreams, including the God Knew vision. I am truly blessed to call you my best friend, and my bride. I love you more than words! Always and forever!

<u>Our Acknowledgements</u>

To our friends who supported us and encouraged us along the way – there are too many to name, but you know who you are. Thank you for sharing this dream, and for your encouragement. It means more than you know.

To our publisher, Tracy Ertl, from Titletown Publishing – thank you for believing in us, our story, and our ministry vision. Thank you for taking a chance on this ordinary couple with a God-inspired story. We will do our best to make sure your faith in us is not in vain.

Our editor, Lori Preuss – thank you for making this book better and for correcting the mistakes we made. We are grateful.

Our attorney, Ben LaFrombois, and his paralegal, Shelly Flunker – thank you for your help and guidance in getting us this far in the trademark, merchandising, and publishing process. We couldn't have done this without your expertise.

Tammy and Bruce Brzeczkowski (and the team) from Dynamic Designs in Pulaski – website design and marketing – God knew what He was doing when He connected us. You are a pure joy to work with and we appreciate your expertise with our new website and the merchandising. Thank you for joining our dream and ministry vision – we appreciate you!

Christy Janeczko from Christy Janeczko Photography for the use of our wedding photos – they were gorgeous, and we love them! Thank you!

Craig Stodola from Craig John Photography for the use of our engagement photos. You were sly behind the camera that day and I was so happy it was you taking our photos. We appreciate you!

TABLE OF CONTENTS

INTRODUCTION

It's me again, Jim, your old friend from *God Knew, Revelations of God's Grace in Unexpected Ways*. It's difficult to believe it's been eight years since I published *God Knew*. Eight years! I wish I could tell you these last nine years since my mom died have been a breeze for me, and there haven't been any big changes in my life since then. If I told you that, however, I'd be lying. And I don't think the word "big" is adequate in describing the magnitude of changes I've experienced.

You've probably already caught on to the biggest change when you read the front cover and saw "Linda Meyer" as a co-author of the book you are holding. And you'd be correct – Linda is my beautiful *wife*.

In the original *God Knew*, you read how God worked in the lives of my dad, my mom, and mine, to guide and direct us to the very places and vocations He planned for us. When we couldn't understand the what, the when, the where, the how, and, most importantly, the why, we took comfort in the two words that became the namesake for these books: God knew.

In this book, you will read a few more stories from my life that pick up at the end of the last book and go until late 2017 when God miraculously brought Linda into my life. You will then read about Linda, an autobiography of sorts, and how our great God worked in her life through all the pain, loneliness, questions, and heartache she walked through to bring her to me. But she didn't walk through that heartache alone – her Savior was right by her side. Linda has her own incredible "God knew" story and you will enjoy getting to know the woman that captured my heart, and now shares my life. We will then tell you how God brought us together, and how He worked some incredible things in our life…more "God knew" moments.

In the introduction of the original *God Knew,* I wrote, "I want to tell you a real-life love story. In a selfish way, I'd like to think the story you are about to read is unique. I know it probably isn't. In fact, I pray that it isn't. I pray that my story is also yours or that it will become yours after you read it."

Friends, that sentiment hasn't changed with the book you are now holding. Linda and I want to tell you another real-life love story – our real-life love story. We hope our story isn't unique, but it likely is. I will also tell you that the story you are about to read will seem almost impossible to believe. If we weren't living it and experiencing it first-hand, we might not believe it, either. I can assure you, everything you are about to read is 100% true. Thankfully, we serve a great God that specializes in doing the impossible.

If you think about it, you can easily think of another real-life love story you've read that seems almost impossible to believe – the Holy Bible. It's difficult to imagine that an omniscient, omnipresent, and all-powerful God created everything out of nothing with the words, "Let there be…" And it was all perfect…perfect until man sinned, and the created rebelled against the Creator. The Bible then describes how, *"For God so loved the world that he gave his one and only Son, that whoever believes in him shall not perish but have eternal life."* John 3:16 (NIV). The Creator became true man, lived a perfect life, then suffered death on a cross to pay the full price for our sins and rebellion. He did this out of love for you and for me. Pastor Shoup has said, "When you really think about what we believe as Christians, it's pretty unbelievable."

While this is indeed a story featuring Linda and me, we aren't the real stars – God is. All the glory and honor go to Him. We want Christ to be the central focus when you are reading this book, just as Linda and I try to keep Christ as the central focus of our lives, and of our marriage. I know it's hard to believe, but even if He hadn't created Linda for me, and His plan was that I remain single the rest of my life, I would still trust in Him.

There is some overlap in our stories, and you might experience a little déjà vu at times. Linda and I wrote our respective portions of this book separately so you could hear our story in our respective voices, and from our respective perspectives. Sometimes it's helpful to see things from both a man's and a woman's point of view.

As Linda and I sat down to write this first sequel to *God Knew*, we realized that the incredible, seemingly unexplainable events in our lives were more than just "God knew" moments – they were God's faithfulness fulfilled. And now you know how we got the subtitle. As we read in 1 Thessalonians 5:24 (ESV), *"He who calls you is faithful; he will surely do it."* Since context is always important, the verse preceding this, verse 23, reads, *"Now may the God of peace himself sanctify you completely, and may your whole spirit and soul and body be kept blameless at the coming of the Lord Jesus Christ."* Hmmm…sanctification. That's quite a "churchy" word, isn't it? To put that in layman's terms, sanctification is the Holy Spirit continuously nurturing and increasing faith in our lives so we can respond to God's love for us in service and love to Him, and others. In short, it's spiritual growth. And whatever we do is out of love for Him and to bring glory to Him, not for any accolades for ourselves or to try and earn our way into heaven or His favor. The Holy Spirit gets all the credit in sanctification because it would be impossible without Him. He gives us the faith to believe, He continuously nurtures that faith and He gives us the power to live out that faith. 1 John 4:19 (ESV) reminds us, *"We love because He first loved us."*

Through it all, the good and the bad, Linda and I have tried to lead lives pleasing to God and to walk in His ways. Since we live in a sinful and sin-filled world, we fail at that every day. Nevertheless, we have tried to remain faithful to God, relying on His promises to be with us and to never forsake us (Hebrews 13:5, paraphrase). We also know that God reveals His grace to us in unexpected ways. And we rest in the assurance that *"He who calls you is faithful; he will surely do it."* 1 Thessalonians 5:24 (ESV).

God knew.

Faithfulness fulfilled.

These two word-pairings are like two incredibly comfortable slippers we love to slip into and walk in every day of our lives. They bring us comfort and they bring us security. They are our fortress of solitude. God knows the end from the beginning (God knew), and the Bible, and our lives, show us time and time again that God is faithful to each and every promise He has ever made, and He will do it, either in this life or the next (faithfulness fulfilled).

We can do nothing in our own strength. We can't even believe in God unless He gives us the faith to believe.

There is comfort in serving a God who keeps all of His promises. There is comfort in serving a God who is all-knowing, ever-present, and all-powerful. Nothing can defeat Him, and we are protected by His grace.

How do we know this? Easy – God told us in the Bible, His Holy Word.

As I did in the introduction to *God Knew*, I want to share with you our core beliefs...beliefs you will hear emphasized again and again in this book. Here they are again as they are still as true for us today as they were eight years ago:

- God is alive, God is more relevant than ever, and God is very intimately involved in your life *("I am the Alpha and the Omega," says the Lord God, "who is and who was and who is to come, the Almighty."* Revelation 1:8 (ESV))

- The Holy Bible, the Ten Commandments, and Jesus Christ are still eternally relevant *("[Jesus said] Heaven and earth will pass away, but my words will not pass away."* Matthew 24:35 (ESV)

- All of us will someday stand before the Holy and Almighty God to give an account of our lives and our faith *("For we will all stand before the judgment seat of God; for it is written, 'As I live, says the Lord, every knee shall bow to me, and every tongue shall confess to God.' So, then each of us will give an account of himself to God."* Romans 14:10 (ESV)

- Believing in Jesus Christ as your Savior is the only way to inherit eternal life in Heaven

- Heaven and hell are both very real

- God does have a plan for your life

- You and your faith will be tested, and therefore strengthened, in this life

- God loves you and wants what is best for you. God is faithful.

If you share these beliefs, then read on. Even if you don't share them, please read on anyway. You are about to experience two incredible love stories – God's love for us, and Linda's and my love for each other. Through both, you will see that God knew and that we have witnessed and continue to experience His faithfulness fulfilled.

PROLOGUE

"Five Life-Changing Words" – A God Knew Recap
and a Preview of this Book

I don't know about you, but whether I love them or hate them depends on the mood I'm in at the time and their quality. The object of my love/hate relationship? Sequels. Some of them are really bad and you wonder why they spent time and money producing them (and you wonder why you spent your time and money watching them). Some are just okay – you can take them or leave them. And some, well, they blow you away. Right now, I'm thinking in particular about *Top Gun Maverick*. In my humble opinion, the sequel was every bit as good as the first movie and might even be better. While *Top Gun Maverick* was thirty years behind the original, it was worth the wait.

It is our hope and prayer that you feel the same way about the book you are holding – that the eight-year wait was worth it. We think this book will blow you away as you see God's faithfulness fulfilled. Two of the main "characters," God and me, are the same. Well, God is the same – He never changes. His grace, His mercy, His love, and His faithfulness are constants. I, on the other hand, have been a poster-boy for change. As you learned in the introduction, the new main character, the heroine of our story, my wife, Linda, is new. Through Linda's story, you will meet several other new characters, too.

A friend gave me some great advice before we went to see *Top Gun Maverick*…watch the original first; certain things will make so much more sense if you do. So, we did; and things did.

The same thing is true with this book – if you haven't read the original *God Knew, Revelations of God's Grace in Unexpected Ways*, I would encourage you to do so first. Certain things will make a lot more sense if you do.

But if you don't have that kind of time, or if you've already read the original and need a refresher, I thought it would be helpful to give you a brief recap of the original *God Knew*, and also give you a "Preview of Coming Attractions" (in keeping with our movie theme in this little chapter introduction).

The other thing I think we all recognize, whether it's in the original or the sequel, we want truly great stories to end with: *"They lived happily ever after."*

Five life-changing words. Five short, easy to remember words: they lived…Happily. Ever. After.

We long to read them at the end of every story (including this one). They embody the emotions we hope to feel at the end of every movie. These are the magic letter combinations that unlock our smiles and warm the deepest places of our hearts.

And don't we long for that for ourselves? Don't we also want to live happily ever after?

But what happens when life doesn't turn out that way? What happens when our happily *ever* after seemingly turns into happily *never* after? It's natural to feel bitter, depressed, betrayed, hopeless, and unloved. We ask, "Why me?" And then, quite possibly, we think about the two words that always follow those five magical words…the end. The end of our happiness, the end of life as we know it, the end of a career, the end of a marriage, the end of good health, the end of my _(you fill in the blank)_ . I suspect you thought of something.

And maybe, because we are now so focused on "the end," we don't do the first two words, "they *lived*."

Because what if, just maybe, "the end" is really the *beginning*? What if "happily ever after" is the start of your spectacular life story, not the end?

Most people absolutely love to hear stories about a man and woman who are high school sweethearts who fell in love, got married right after college, have fulfilling jobs they love for over 25 years, own a large two-story Victorian home with a white picket fence, have 3 amazing children, 5 wonderful grandchildren, a quirky little Beagle named Sparky, and are looking forward to retirement coming up.

A story like that certainly qualifies for "they lived happily ever after."

Or watch virtually any Hallmark or GAC Family movie and you know the plot: boy meets girl, boy and girl dislike each other, boy and girl find a common bond, there is a misunderstanding about an hour and forty minutes into the movie that breaks up said boy and girl, the misunderstanding is resolved with a few minutes left, and we see the boy and girl kissing as the movie ends, with snow gently falling (even in the middle of July).

It's like living a dream.

You might be smiling right now and agreeing... Happily. Ever. After.

Well, you know from reading *God Knew, Revelations of God's Grace in Unexpected Ways*, that my actual life doesn't look anything like the two scenarios I just outlined. Life happened, and my plans changed. As the years went by, and the distance between my reality and my ideal life widened, my dreams faded, and hopes of happily ever after ended. I was just trying to make the best of my life for the next several decades until the end. Perhaps you know exactly what I'm talking about?

It's difficult to get to your "happily ever after" when you can't even get started. For me, my plans all started with the perfect woman.

If you look up the poster child for the Yiddish proverb, "Man plans, God laughs," you'll find my picture.

To be fair, if God had revealed His actual plans for my life when I was a teenager, *I* would have laughed. Or, more likely, doubted Him.

Now, please don't feel bad for me. Just because my dreams didn't become my reality doesn't mean my life has been terrible. It hasn't. As you know, I have lived a great life that most people would trade for in a second. I have been, and continue to be, incredibly blessed.

There is no way I could have known the real path that would eventually lead me to my bride, or the fact my perfect woman would show up decades later than I expected.

But God knew.

Part of God's plan was to give me a blessing that most people don't get. And, if they do get it, they often miss it.

As you read in the original *God Knew*, I am an only child, raised in a Christian home by God-fearing parents who taught me morals, values, integrity, and character. I learned about doing things right and doing the right thing. God gave me the incredible opportunity to honor my parents and take care of them in their old age. Both of my parents had health challenges, financial challenges, and many other struggles. I don't know what their "happily ever after" dreams consisted of, but I do know they deeply loved each other. And God.

As you know, my high school dreams of a sweetheart fizzled, so I deferred those dreams until college. They didn't materialize then, either. I just couldn't get to my starting point: no high school sweetheart (not even a date), and no college girlfriend on my arm at graduation. God had a plan that kept me single, and in my hometown, so I could care for my parents. I was offered a nice full-time job after college at the bank I was working for part-time, purchased a home, and moved my parents in with me. I did my best to give them a happily ever after.

I dated a few women over the years, but nothing ever felt quite right. I began to doubt if God had made "the one" for me. Marriage is a big deal to me; I only wanted to be married once. A lot of people told me my standards were too high. I disagreed. I have always believed it is better to be single than with the wrong person.

In the meantime, my career progressed, and I rose in the banking ranks, going from the mailroom in 1987 to the position of bank president in 2008. I got involved in my church. I volunteered for many community organizations. I cultivated life-long friendships with family-oriented, Christian couples. I put more focus on my family relationships. I tried everything I could to take my focus off the intense loneliness I felt, even though I was always around people.

But while my career, community efforts, and friendships were on the rise, my parents' health was on the decline. Alzheimer's continued to erode Dad's mind. Blood clots, a heart attack, and a stroke weakened his body. Doctors advised us to put him in a skilled nursing facility, so we did. Mom stayed living with me and our relationship deepened. She became my best friend. Over the years, her body continued to weaken due to a plethora of issues. It's difficult to watch a loved one slowly decline, knowing the inevitable will happen, no matter how many prayers you pray, and how many deals you try to make with God.

The one thing that never, and I mean never, declined in my parents was their faith in God. Even in the most trying circumstances, they continued to love Him, trust Him, and look to Him for everything. I wish I could say the same for myself. There were times I doubted, and my anger at God got the better of me (for a little while, anyway).

I never did ask them when it happened, but I know at some point they both came to the realization their happily ever after was coming, but not in this earthly life. Through their Holy Spirit-inspired faith in Jesus as their Savior, they knew they would spend eternity in Heaven with the One who loves them the most – the One who had never left them nor forsaken them – the One who died for them. They knew their future included pain-free bodies that would never again know the ravages and disappointments a sin-filled world brings. They knew death, the end of this life, was just the beginning of their happily ever after.

Dad went to Heaven in August 2012. Mom followed him in February 2014. At that point, I thought my life had likely also ended. I had no real plans beyond their life. Who knew their "the end" would be the reason I could start to "live"?

God knew.

Shortly after Mom died, I felt inspired to write *God Knew: Revelations of God's Grace in Unexpected Ways*. It's the true story about my life and my parents' lives that reveals God's perfect grace and perfect timing, often in ways we don't understand until later. It was another way for me to honor them and God.

My 29-year career at the bank became intolerable. Enough was enough. I wasn't happy anymore. I dreaded going to work. I disliked my boss. I didn't know what to do. But God knew. Through a series of seemingly unrelated circumstances, that were all part of God's plan, a new position at a new bank in town opened that was far better. Hmmm... creating something where there was nothing – God is famous for that. Almost seven years later, I am incredibly happy in my career again. What I thought was an end, was really a better beginning.

Once I got the silly notion out of my head that my chance for true love had passed me by, I signed up for various online dating sites and even hired a professional matchmaker. I knew I had a lot to offer the right woman – if I could just find her. My standards had not diminished over the years. I created a list of what I would want in my "perfect" woman. Upon completion, there were 67 qualities on that list. Once again, people told me my standards were too high. I won't elaborate on those dating experiences, but after a year of frustrations, I decided to give up on finding a wife. I would be okay just being a loving, Christian friend to all those around me. I resolved to make myself content with my new plan of remaining single forever.

I believe at that point God was rolling on Heaven's floor, laughing. God knew what I was going through at that time was "wait gain."

In November 2017, I was working in my family room. Hallmark Christmas movies were playing in the background. Commercials normally annoy me, and I kept hearing the ad from eHarmony repeatedly telling how it was a "free communication weekend." After what seemed like 100 eHarmony commercials, I finally decided to log on and check it out. I went into this with a skeptical "What's the worst that could happen?" attitude, when God was already working His plan to answer the question, "What's the *best* that could happen?"

His answer: Linda (a/k/a the girl in the red scarf – foreshadowing).

Within a short period of time, we discovered we had so much in common, and had lived somewhat parallel lives. We discovered that maybe true love hadn't passed either of us by. We discovered this could be the answer to a very long period of waiting and hoping and praying.

I believe at that point, God just smiled.

Linda met the vast majority of my 67 qualities, and I met the vast majority of hers. We are so thankful neither one of us compromised. Soon, five life-changing words were spoken: "I'm in love with you!"

Then, on May 18, 2018, five more life-changing words: "Linda, will you marry me?" We were married on November 3, 2018, at her church and did an Affirmation of Vows at my church just two weeks later, in front of the same altar my parents exchanged their wedding vows in 1965. Again, five life-changing words, "Do you take this man/woman?" And then, finally, FINALLY, "You may kiss your bride!"

So, friend, don't give up! You never know what God has planned. But God knew. Hebrews 13:5 (ESV), states, *"...be content with what you have, for He has said, 'I will never leave you nor forsake you.'"* Jeremiah 29:11 (NIV), reminds us, *"For I know the plans I have for you,"* *declares the LORD, "plans to prosper you and not to harm you, plans to give you hope and a future."*

Here are more encouraging five-word phrases that are "eternal life" changing:

- Your life is not over

- Endings can create exciting beginnings

- God's timing is always perfect

- God is good and faithful

- Jesus loves you so much

- Jesus died for your sins

- Jesus rose from the grave

- Jesus is coming back again

God will answer your prayers. But I'd be remiss if I didn't tell you it might not be the answer you want. His answer might be no and you may never know "why" this side of heaven. And if that is His answer, rest assured that while you might feel lonely, you are never really alone. Jesus is always right by your side, walking with you no matter what you are going through. Even when you can't feel Him or see Him, He is still right there. The depth of His love for you is unfathomable. Your happily ever after will come, either in this life or the next. Hopefully in both. And, at Heaven's gate, these are the five words that will mean the most: "Well done, good & faithful servant."

Linda and I know how blessed we are, and that God had the

perfect plan…and perfect timing. We are confident the epitaph to our amazing love story will be, both now and in eternity, "they lived happily ever after."

As you might expect, there is a lot more to the story than the "preview" you just read.

And now, the sequel, *God Knew, Faithfulness Fulfilled*, our feature presentation…

CHAPTER 1
WHERE WE LEFT OFF...

⁸ Love never ends. As for prophecies, they will pass away; as for tongues, they will cease; as for knowledge, it will pass away. ⁹ For we know in part and we prophesy in part, ¹⁰ but when the perfect comes, the partial will pass away. ¹¹ When I was a child, I spoke like a child, I thought like a child, I reasoned like a child. When I became a man, I gave up childish ways. ¹² For now we see in a mirror dimly, but then face to face. Now I know in part; then I shall know fully, even as I have been fully known.

¹³ So now faith, hope, and love abide, these three; but the greatest of these is love. 1 Corinthians 13: 8-13 (ESV)

When we left off at the end of *God Knew, Revelations of God's Grace in Unexpected Ways,* it had been only several months since my mom died. The end of forty-five years together with my best friend was incredibly difficult to grasp and there was nothing I could do about it, except keep moving forward. I was in severe emotional pain. I missed her so much and my tears were flowing freely on a daily basis. Admittedly, sometimes they still do – nine years later. One of my goals in writing *God Knew* was to help people deal with their grief. I said, "If even one person is helped by the words of this book, this entire project was worth it." I reiterated that to a friend of mine, Kelly, shortly before *God Knew* was self-published. She asked me, "Did it help *you* to write it?" I hadn't thought of it in those terms before, but she was absolutely right – it did help me to write it. When I acknowledged that, she smiled and said, "Well, there is your one." I do pray it has helped you, and many others, too.

After *God Knew* was released, I wrote many blog posts that chronicled my journey through grief, and some general thoughts about dealing with life. Notice that I said, "*through* grief." Whatever you are going through right now, friend, you will get *through* it. But you don't go through anything alone – you do have a God that walks through every fire, trial, temptation, and tear, with you. I am living proof that with God's help, you will get through this, whatever "this" is. You've read the "preview of coming attractions;" you also know "through" is possible.

One of those blog posts was titled, "Where We Left Off" and I'd like to share it with you here, as the title fits in with a book sequel, and it also ties in nicely to Kelly's comment, "Well, there is your one." Here is the post (keep in mind I wrote this almost three years after Mom died, in December 2016, so there is a Christmas theme to it):

"Martina.

Sometimes one name says it all. And if you follow music, and I say the name, 'Martina,' you know exactly who I'm talking about.

I have been a big fan of country music singer, Martina McBride since she started her career. She has had quite a few hits that share a very important message. The following song is no exception.

Written to honor, support, and encourage our military members and their families, 'We'll Pick Up Where We Left Off,' is another great song with a great message. I especially like the lyrics to the refrain which encourages the families to not say "good-bye" but rather, to say "good night." The refrain points to an anticipation of getting to say "hello" again and picking up where things left off.

The song itself has a nice thought for those military members leaving for duty, something like, 'We are not going to say goodbye, because goodbye can sometimes mean an end to something. Rather, let's just say good night because that means we hope to see each other in the new day. And when you finally come home, we'll be there to greet you at the door with a hello and to welcome you home. We'll pick up where we left off, the feelings will be just as strong (like you never left), and life will get back to normal again.' Beautiful thoughts, especially this time of year.

It's Christmas – a time to once again focus on the birth of our Lord and Savior.

I wonder if God maybe said something similar to Jesus when Jesus was leaving the glories of Heaven to become a little baby, 'Jesus, we're not going to say goodbye. You know what You have to do: go down to Earth, live a perfect life, and die a cruel death on the cross to pay for the sins of all mankind. But don't worry, Jesus, I've got this all the way. I will raise You to life again on the third day. And a few weeks after that, You will ascend back to Heaven. We'll pick up where We left off and start preparing places for all those who believe in You and are saved.' I can just picture the Father standing at the entrance to Heaven, waiting for Jesus to return triumphant, giving Him a big smile and hug, and saying, 'Hello, Jesus. Welcome Home.' Part of me wants to think they also gave each other a victorious 'high five.'

Sometimes I get some weird thoughts. For instance, I think about Mom every day (that's not the weird thought). I miss her every single day. I still hurt every single day. My love for Mom has not diminished in the least. But then I get worried about Mom in Heaven. Sounds goofy, right? Why would I worry about Mom being in Heaven? After all, there are sights and sounds beyond our comprehension. Her soul is with relatives, friends, and all the saints that have gone before us, the entire company of Heaven, being in the very presence of God, perhaps even having a nice conversation with Jesus. Eternal love and joy and peace are all around her. No more sin, no more pain, no more tears, no more death. I am so happy for Mom and so thankful the Holy Spirit sustained her faith until the end. But I get a little worried at times that with all the glory and splendor Heaven has to offer that Mom has moved on without me. And what will happen when God calls me Home - will Mom even remember me? As I said, weird thoughts, right?

Then I re-visited the refrain from Martina's song. I picture what I hope will happen at the moment I take my last breath on earth: Jesus will take me by the hand and walk me safely through the valley of the shadow of death. We continue on and I can see Heaven. As we get closer, there she is, my mom, standing by the proverbial pearly gates. My Dad is standing there next to her. Jesus somehow beat me back to Heaven and He and the Father are also there. They are all smiling and happy. Mom gives me a great big hug that seems to last for eternity, then Dad. Finally, Jesus stretches out His loving arms and nail-pierced hands and gives me the biggest hug while saying, 'Hello, Jim. Welcome Home. Well done, thou good and faithful servant.' I believe that is the same way He greeted both Mom and Dad.

And no matter how many years pass from February 25, 2014, when Mom died, until the day God calls me Home, I believe Mom and I will pick up right where we left off. After all, Love lasts forever.

I pray the same holds true for you and your loved ones - a joyous, happy reunion that picks up right where you left off.

Here is another thought: maybe as Jesus was leaving Heaven, the Father didn't say goodbye, but said 'Good night.' And maybe that was more than a farewell greeting – maybe it was also encouragement for what Jesus had to do and a preview of things to come.

Because, for us, that first Christmas wasn't just a good night.

It was a great night.

The best night.

A silent night.

A Holy night.

A night Divine.

A night in Bethlehem about 2,000 years ago, when all was calm and all was bright and a Baby was born in a stable, wrapped in swaddling cloths, and laid in a manger because there wasn't room at the inn. A Baby born to Joseph and Mary. The Savior of all who believe in Him by the power of the Holy Spirit has come to earth! Joy to the world!

Christ is born!

Immanuel (God with us).

Jesus.

*The one name above all other names that really does say it all -
the only name we need to be saved eternally."*

As Kelly told me that day, "Well, there is your one." I'm here to tell you today, "Well, there [Jesus] is *your* One." He is the One Who has gotten me this far. When we left off, I was sort of a mess and felt I had no purpose in my life. In some ways, I felt alone. But I wasn't. I never was. Jesus walked with me as I walked through intense grief in the valley of the shadow of my parents' deaths. He is the One Who walked with me through a job change, online dating, and various other life circumstances. Ultimately, He is the One Who led me to Linda. The road was winding, and many times I couldn't even see the next step ahead. There were times I wanted to give up, and just let go. Thankfully, the One I trust in proved His faithfulness and never let go of me. I know my Savior has traveled every path before me, and He knows the way. He is THE Way (and the Truth, and the Life). We can only get to the Father through Him. My parents knew that, and they passed their faith down to me.

A politician, addressing a group of grieving military families, once said, "There will come a day when the thought of your loved one brings a smile to your lips before it brings a tear to your eye." I can assure you, when I think of Mom, a smile comes to my lips way more often than the tears come to my eye (although, the tears do still come).

Lorraine Emilie Meyer was my one and only earthly Mom. Ralph William Meyer was my one and only earthly Dad.

Lorraine. Mom.

Ralph. Dad.

Jesus. Savior.

Heaven. Home.

It turns out one name really does say it all.

At a time known only to God, He will call me from this earth to my Heavenly Home. He will call me by my name, James William

Meyer – the same name given to me in my Baptism to mark me as one who belongs to Him.

And I know when that time happens, and I get to Heaven, all three of us will pick up right where we left off. Love lasts forever. *"For the LORD is good; his steadfast love endures forever, and his faithfulness to all generations."* Psalm 100:5 (ESV).

CHAPTER 2
ENOUGH IS ENOUGH

"Philip said to him, 'Lord, show us the Father, and it is enough for us.'" – John 14:8 (NIV)

Overall, I would consider myself a very loyal person. I am loyal to my faith, my family, my friends, and my employer. I even try to be loyal to myself and my convictions, trying to live out the old adage, "To thine own self be true." And while I don't get my way as often as I like, I do probably get it more than I deserve. I try desperately to be grateful for the blessings I have, and to consider what I have "enough." After all, my Confirmation verse, Hebrews 13:5 (ESV), starts with, *"Be content with what you have…"* All too often, though, my actions show it isn't, and I'm not.

The Golden Rule says to do unto others as you would have them do unto you. The Golden Result says that people will usually treat us the same way we treat them. For example: treat them with loyalty, and they will likely treat you with loyalty. It's nice when things work out that way, but let's face it, we live in an imperfect world.

In 2016, my life was at major cross-roads. I wasn't happy at my employer anymore. The culture had shifted drastically, and I could feel the loyalty balance shifting. I didn't feel secure in my job, and my twenty-nine years of loyalty were put to the test. I thought, "enough is enough," I need something else. My possibilities were limited – Shawano is an over-banked community, and the job options for me were less than slim, bordering on none. I felt unbelievably trapped between a rock and a hard place and didn't know what my next move would be.

But God knew.

A long-time coworker, who at that time was also a friend, had left that organization about a year earlier, after almost 25 years of loyalty. He found a great job with a great bank, Denmark State Bank. We kept in touch periodically and he would tell me how happy he was, and

I would tell him how unhappy I was. He loved his new boss, John Rehn, and suggested that John and I meet for coffee. Networking with quality people is something I enjoy, so I agreed. The three of us met at Perkins in Green Bay one afternoon. The in-person John far exceeded the hype. He is a solid Christian who loves Jesus and his family. He also demonstrated loyalty to both, and to his employer and employees, and that was something that drew me like a moth to a flame.

However, Denmark State Bank did not have a branch in Shawano, and that is where the vast majority of my loyal customers are located. For me to move to another market didn't feel right; my customers were loyal to me, and I owed them that loyalty in return. John and the bank president, Scot, both saw value in having me on the Denmark team and equal value in my client base. How were we ever going to make this work?

God knew.

I had never heard of a loan production office (LPO) before and Denmark had never attempted one, but they were willing to give it a try. They made me a job offer with the condition they would open an LPO in Shawano so I could continue to serve my clients locally. It wasn't a full-service branch, but it was better than nothing.

I had worked with my portfolio manager/assistant, Annette, for over 25 years. You read a little about her in the original *God Knew*. She is more "loyal friend" than a coworker. She was also not happy, and not feeling the loyalty in return, after 35 years of loyal service to our prior bank. So, I made a deal with John to make the Shawano LPO a package deal. John made Annette an offer to join Denmark and continue to work with me. Surprisingly, she declined – that is how strong her loyalty is; she had worked *for* the bank longer than she had worked *with* me. But God knew we should keep that position open and available. Thankfully, after a few months of continued unhappiness, Annette changed her mind and decided to join Denmark.

Our loyalty to our clients was not misplaced. The vast majority of them followed us to our new bank. Within a year, we expanded from an LPO to a limited-service branch. Then, within 3 years of the LPO,

Scot purchased a former bank building for us to have a full-service branch in Shawano. That branch is literally two blocks away from our home (and that will tie in nicely with the story about our home purchase, *Home Sweet Home*).

Since 2016, John and his wife, Michele, have become very close friends with Linda and me. They are such good people, with a strong faith in God, and a love for Jesus, their family, and their friends. We are blessed to call them our friends.

The subtitle of this book is "Faithfulness Fulfilled." As I was writing this chapter, I wondered if loyalty and faithfulness are the same thing. I discovered that in a wide sense, they are. In a narrower sense, there are some subtle differences, with the main one being faithfulness has some religious connotations given the root word, faith. And faithfulness is a great and accurate way to describe God's relationship with us.

How many times in the Old Testament did the children of Israel demonstrate unfaithfulness to God? Many. Conversely, how many times did God demonstrate His continued and enduring faithfulness to them? Countless. As I look back at my life, I can see clearly how faithful God has been to me. Good times, bad times, *meh* times – God was always there, always faithful. I often didn't understand what was happening, but I trusted in the One who did.

God knew I wasn't happy at my prior employer. God knew that from my perspective, there didn't seem to be a way out. God also knows and sees what we don't. That is where faith comes in. God has always been faithful to work things out for me in the past. Always. I need to have faith and confidence that He will fulfill His promise and will continue to work *all* things together for my good in the future. Even if I don't get my way, I need to trust His way. I read a definition of faith that said, "Faith is not believing God can; it is knowing that He will."

Enough is enough. I felt that way in 2016. Something had to change. I couldn't keep on with that untenable situation. God knew I needed a change.

Enough is enough. In Bethlehem, around 2,000 years ago, God sent His only begotten Son to be born of a virgin, to live a perfect life free of sin, and to die on a cross to take the penalty for my sin and for the sins of the whole world. God knew we needed a Savior.

Enough is enough. Three days after His crucifixion, the crucified Jesus rose from the dead, conquering sin, death, and the power of the devil once and for all. He ascended to heaven and sits at the right hand of God, interceding for us as our great High Priest. And like us, He waits. What does Jesus wait for? He waits for the time when the Father says...

"Enough is enough." Enough pain, enough tears, enough sadness, enough suffering, enough sin, enough rebellion, enough unfaithfulness. Jesus is waiting for the Father to tell Him to go and get His faithful bride, the Church, and bring her home to heaven for the wedding of all weddings. Revelation 21:1-8 (ESV) says,

> *"¹Then I saw a new heaven and a new earth, for the first heaven and the first earth had passed away, and the sea was no more. ²And I saw the holy city, new Jerusalem, coming down out of heaven from God, prepared as a bride adorned for her husband. ³And I heard a loud voice from the throne saying, "Behold, the dwelling place of God is with man. He will dwell with them, and they will be his people, and God himself will be with them as their God. ⁴He will wipe away every tear from their eyes, and death shall be no more, neither shall there be mourning, nor crying, nor pain anymore, for the former things have passed away."*
>
> *⁵And he who was seated on the throne said, "Behold, I am making all things new." Also, he said, "Write this down, for these words are trustworthy and true." ⁶And he said to me, "It is done! I am the Alpha and the Omega, the beginning and the end. To the thirsty I will give from the spring of the water of life without payment. ⁷The one who conquers will have this heritage, and I will be his God and he will be my son. ⁸But as for the cowardly, the faithless, the detestable, as for murderers, the sexually immoral, sorcerers, idolaters, and all liars, their portion will be in the lake that burns with fire and sulfur, which is the second death."*

God's timing is always perfect. At the right time, He provided the right opportunity for a new job for me. At the right time, He provided a Savior, Who was more than enough to defeat our enemies. At the right time, our Savior will return. God's Word doesn't tell us that day or the hour when the Father will say, "Enough is enough," but He has given you enough time and enough means to be ready for that moment. The fact you are still alive and reading this proves you still have enough time to know that God is more than enough. Through the Holy Spirit, He even provides enough faith for you to believe and be saved. In heaven, you will never want for anything, you will be with our Heavenly Father, and you will always have more than enough.

CHAPTER 3

THE GIRL IN THE RED...SCARF??

If you have ever participated in online dating, what I'm about to tell you is likely very relatable. If you haven't tried it, but are thinking about it, then consider yourself warned. If you have found your "one," consider yourself blessed you don't have to deal with this.

While online dating obviously worked for Linda and me, it is not for the faint of heart. You need to be prepared for lies, deception, disappointment, and heartache. Thankfully, I was able to close all my profiles and cancel my subscriptions over 5 years ago – I pray the experience of online dating has gotten somewhat better since then.

Some sites provide a little more flexibility in communicating and obtaining information than others. Being the cheapskate that I am, I focused my attention on the less expensive sites but still created limited profiles on some other, more expensive sites.

The first thing to think about is time. Consider this: if you are single and tired of spending endless, lonely hours scrolling through your social media feeds, well, have I got a deal for you, friend: sign up for online dating and spend endless, still lonely hours scrolling through your potential matches. It. Is. Exhausting. Then, for the next thrill – send a message to somebody you are interested in and wait for their reply. And wait, and wait, and wait… You can tell they read your message; you can see they checked out your profile. And yet, crickets. Common courtesy really isn't that common anymore – neither is courtesy. Your thoughts of, "What is wrong with some people?" quickly turn to, "What is wrong with *me*?" I know; I was there.

Determined to not spend my life alone, I did the next logical thing – spent thousands, yes, thousands, of dollars on a professional matchmaking service. You will read later how cheap I really am when it comes to spending money on myself, so this "solution" is so incredibly un-Jim-like. Contrary to online dating where you self-assess, the professionals take the time to do personal interviews, delve into your likes and dislikes, get a handle on your preferences, and then set to work on finding "the one" for you from their extensive client base. They promised at least two in-person dates each month, and they arranged everything. While I met several nice women and there was mutual interest, none of them were close to me geographically – they didn't want a long-distance relationship and neither did I (foreshadowing). However, the majority of the women they matched me with didn't even fit the criteria I said I was looking for. I was, once again, disappointed.

At that point, there was a woman in Shawano I had known for years, and we volunteered for a local service organization. We started to hang out, go to events, have dinners together, etc. We both knew this wasn't a long-term "love connection," but it was fun to "feel normal" and have somebody to do fun things with. During one of our phone conversations, she referred to a "list" she had created years ago of some qualities she was looking for in her husband. I had never really thought of creating my own list (the online dating profiles and professional matchmaking covered this, but I had never made my own list). If memory serves me correctly, she had something like five things on her list.

Allow me to digress for just a minute (again, if you are single, perhaps you can relate to what I'm about to share) – you might think that the most difficult thing to hear when you are single and looking is for somebody to say, "No" when you ask them out. When you are young, confident, and view the world with wide-eyed optimism, you typically don't have a problem just asking somebody out. You may be a little scared of how you'll feel if they say, "No" – you might be hurt and devastated. But you know if they say, "Yes" you will be happy and excited. Now, if you get to the point I was in life, the pendulum swung 180 degrees. The "No" didn't hurt me anymore – I was firmly and fully expecting the "No." What scared me the most was if a woman actually said, "Yes." Why was I scared? Well, if she said yes, now I had to actually plan a date. If she said yes, I'd wonder what was wrong with her since every other woman said no. I'm old-fashioned – if I asked her out, then it's up to me to plan the date, including the restaurant, entertainment, etc. I also had to break out of my naturally introverted shell, dust off my social skills, prepare for engaging conversation, etc. Then, what to wear, what time to arrive, how to end the date, etc. It's exhausting. I stopped asking not because of a potential "No," but because of an improbable "Yes."

So where am I going in this digression? The rejection stopped hurting. The loneliness started to become acceptable, and even expected. Did anything hurt? Yup. What hurt the most when I was older and still single were the well-intentioned words from people around me, "You are such a great guy. You have so much to offer a woman. I just don't understand why God hasn't blessed you with a wife."

Ouch.

I knew those words weren't meant to hurt or harm, but that doesn't mean they didn't pierce my heart.

I knew those words were spoken out of care and concern, but that doesn't mean they didn't hurt.

It could be they hurt so much because I knew something those well-intentioned people didn't know: I had repeated those same words to myself every night I went home to an empty house, and many nights while soaking my pillow with tears. "God, why haven't you blessed me with a wife yet? I'm a pretty good guy. What's wrong with me?" Those prayers appeared to fall on seemingly deaf ears.

It's difficult to accept something when there really isn't a clear answer to the question: Why?

But, once again, God knew!

There was also a little bit of irony in play here. I would often tell people that my perfect wife was not hanging out in bars on a Saturday night, but she would be at home, snuggled up on her couch, watching Hallmark movies, and wondering why she hadn't met her forever love yet, either. But if we were both at home watching movies and eating popcorn, how would we ever meet? God knew.

May I now share one little-used word with you that was pointed out to me well after I met Linda, but really applies to the "being single" season I was navigating? That word is: placeholder.

My best friend growing up, Paul Frisque (you read about our friendship and his incredibly helpful emails to me in the original *God Knew*) is a long-time teacher in the Wisconsin Evangelical Lutheran Synod (WELS), and he and his family still live in the Milwaukee, Wisconsin area. Paul had received a Divine Call to serve at a church in Michigan. He and his family didn't know what to do so they did what they always do: they prayed and prayed and prayed. Eventually, Paul declined the Call in order to stay serving at his then-current school. The congregation that called him then called a different teacher and that person accepted the call. I don't know if it was the pastor or the principal at the Michigan school that told Paul later on (paraphrased): "Paul, don't feel bad about not accepting the Call. We know now that you were just a placeholder. The teacher we have now, who is the best fit for the position, would not have been able to accept the Call if we had issued it earlier. We needed to call you, and have you take the necessary time to deliberate and decline the Call, in order for this man to be ready. There were some things God was working on in his life to get him ready to accept our Call. Everything works out in God's plan and in His timing."

So, with that in mind, while you are in your season of waiting, consider this hindsight view of my same season:

- My Mom and Dad (taking them in and taking care of them) – placeholders
- Online dating – placeholder
- Professional matchmaking (and the good and bad dates I experienced) – placeholder
- The woman in Shawano – placeholder

God had more work that He needed to do in my life to prepare me for the "forever love" He knew I wanted. He knew He had more work to do with Linda, too, to get her ready, and you will read about her placeholders, too.

In reality, these were more than just placeholders; they were also teaching moments. I learned things about life, about other people, about relationships, and most importantly, about myself.

From my parents, I learned that relationships and marriage are hard. You are not always going to get along with your spouse. You will have disagreements and you may have screaming fights. Communication is important. In-laws can be a real pain and complicate things. But, as you read in *God Knew*, I also learned from them that a solid marriage is built on the firm foundation of Jesus Christ. I learned that worshipping together and praying together brings you closer, despite the differences. I learned that fights don't equal failure, and that love is sometimes not a feeling – it's a decision.

From my online dating, I learned that not everybody is in this for the same reasons and that some people's self-awareness is incredibly flawed. Who they are in real life is nothing like who they portray themselves to be online. Online lies are easy to hide behind, and what you see on social media is not always what you get.

From the professional matchmaking dating, I learned to be comfortable with who I am. As I told you in *God Knew*, I am, at the end of the day, just Jim. Like me, don't like me, it really doesn't matter – what you see is what you get. These experiences also honed and refined what I was looking for in a wife. I met some women with good qualities I had not considered, and I met some women that exhibited qualities I definitely didn't want in my wife. Basically, I was focusing more on my likes and dislikes.

From the Shawano woman, I decided to make a list. But not just any list – I was going to make *THE* list! Okay, true confession time – since there didn't seem to be a good answer to the well-meaning comments and the "Why?" I mentioned above, I was going to *make* the answer, and that answer would be a list to end all lists. I've always known I have high standards for my wife. I plan on being married only once, and if I'm only doing this once, it will be to the absolutely right woman. And, because of my love of spreadsheets, a hand-written list just wouldn't do. Enter Excel.

Over the next several days, I began to develop my list. I started with my "must haves" – these are the non-negotiables. Then there are the "needs" – very similar to must-haves, but not as high on the priority list. Finally, the "wants" – qualities and characteristics that would just enhance an already solid relationship built on the must-haves and the needs. Since I never do anything in a simple way, the final list had a total of 67 qualities. Yes, you read that correctly, 67. (I share that list of qualities and characteristics in a later chapter.) I was now prepared for the heart-piercing question, "Why are you still single?" with a definitive, "Here are 67 reasons why!! I'm not going to lower my standards." I might be alone for the rest of my life, but I still have my list (I mean, *standards*)! There was a bit of hollow comfort in that.

Now, for all of you weekend psychologists and psychotherapists reading this, let me share my own self-awareness assessment: at that time, I was 48 years old, never married, still a virgin, with limited experience with relationships. I realized I was likely going to get married to a divorced woman with some kids, and possibly grandkids. So, with all of that lurking in my subconscious, the most obvious thing to do is create an impossible list so the anxiety and insecurities I was feeling would never need to be exposed. I just knew that I would be single the rest of my life because of my list – and now I finally had the justification why.

I'm sure when my list was completed, God just smiled, and perhaps even chuckled. Why?

Because God knew…better. He knew He created someone wonderful in 1970 and that He was working His masterful plan since then, placeholders and all.

Friends, we serve a great God. We serve a God who loves us, whose timing is impeccable. Nothing is impossible for God – not even my list of 67 qualities. I could have made a list of 670 qualities, and He still would have smiled that same smile. He knew the one He kept for me because He made her for me.

At long last, we finally get to the namesake of the title of this chapter.

It was a cold afternoon on Sunday, November 26, 2017 (three days after Thanksgiving). I was in my family room working on a project on my computer. I had the television on like I normally do, with Hallmark Christmas movies playing in the background. I don't recall the movies they aired, but what caught my attention were the incessant commercials for eHarmony with the founder smilingly proclaiming, "It's free communication weekend! Message your matches for free!!"

Free is a very enticing word for a cheapskate, especially this cheapskate. No matter what you are doing, when you are cheap, the word "free" breaks through. (Side note: I often refer to myself as a "generous cheapskate." I don't mind donating money to charities or helping someone in need. I do mind spending money on myself. So, spending thousands on the professional matchmaking service was so out of character for me. In his speech at our wedding reception, Pastor Shoup said he was talking to my then-manager, John, about my thriftiness. John told Pastor that I am, and I quote, "tighter than bark on a tree." He is not too far from the truth!)

Anyway, I had a profile established on eHarmony, but since it was more expensive than the other sites, I wasn't a paid member. I thought, "I need a break anyway. I'll log on and check it out. What's the worst that can happen?"

Our great God once again smiled, because He knew He was about to change my question to, "What's the *best* that can happen?" and my long-standing cry of "How long, O Lord?" was about to receive the Divine answer of, "Now!"

Sorry – one more quick digression; one additional thing about online dating. Back when I was doing this, for some sites, if you weren't a paid member, the pictures of your matches would look like they were participating in a federal government witness protection program. Seriously. You could slightly make out the hair and some clothing, but facial features were incredibly blurred. You could, however, still read their profile. There is something about the policy that I like – judge the person first for their inside character, not their outside appearance.

Now, back to my story. I logged into eHarmony. The first match to come up was a woman named Linda. Again, I couldn't see her face clearly, but I could tell she was wearing a red scarf and had blonde hair. I knew I had seen that red scarf on another dating site. Much like Columbo, I was determined to put my detective skills to work and find her on the other site. And I did. I could see Linda's pictures. What drew me in was her incredible smile and her eyes.

I read Linda's profile. She didn't know this until we started writing this book, but I did a copy and paste of her profile so I could have easy access to it in the future. Here is a portion of what I read:

Basics:

Occupation – Executive Assistant

Education – Some college

School – North Central University

Religion – Christian

Politics – Very Conservative

Lifestyle:

Smoking – Never

Drinking – Never

Kids – I don't have kids but I might want kids

Pets – She likes cats, dogs, horses

What I'm most passionate about:

I am passionate about walking in faith & God's grace daily. I love having a listening ear, being an encouraging voice, or just being "there" for others when they need it most. I just want to be a blessing and make a difference in the lives of those with whom I interact. I love to sing and perform and am very involved in the music and drama ministry at my church. Other areas of passion include traveling, reading, spending time with friends and family…music, coffee, and sushi.

I typically spend my leisure time:

Reading, watching TV/movies, spending time with friends.

The most important thing I'm looking for in a person:

Someone who is genuine, honest about his faith/beliefs, trustworthy; a man of integrity who knows what he wants in life and doesn't compromise his beliefs to get there. An Ephesians 5 man.

The most influential person in my life

My pastor. He's been there for me and my family for the last 30+ years and he has never wavered in his love for my family and never shied away from speaking truth in love. His message and his walk have always been consistent.

The one thing I wish more people would notice about me

That I have a kind, caring and compassionate heart, and I would love to share it with someone deserving of it.

A little more about me

I believe God has a call on my life to be used to reach out and be an encouragement to women who are hurting and in need, and to eliminate Biblical poverty across the world. I volunteer (remotely) with Proverbs 31 Ministries out of North Carolina in their social media department, whose sole purpose is to do just that.

3 best life skills

- Being a good friend
- Volunteering my time
- Appreciating art and culture

3 things I'm thankful for

- Salvation
- Family
- Friends

5 things I can't live without

- God
- Family
- Friends
- My Dog
- Coffee

How my friends describe me

- Caring
- Happy
- Loyal
- Energetic

I know, right? How could I not respond to this profile? After all, when I looked at the date they matched us, it was November 26, 2016. Yes – a recent match! It was exactly that day! It was exactly that same… wait a minute. This is 2017. They matched us a *year* ago and I missed it! A girl this nice, this special, this wonderful was surely taken by now. My joy quickly turned to disappointment. I had lost out again.

I tried to console my disappointment with this thought, "Well, she lives in Oak Creek, which is about 2 ½ hours away from Shawano. Many of the girls I had a date with through the professional matchmaking company were from the Milwaukee area and it was the distance that was the main problem (or convenient excuse). This would have been a long-distance relationship so it's probably for the best we don't connect."

Sometimes I wonder if God wants to just take a baseball bat and whack me upside the head. He could if He wanted to. Thankfully, in this case, He used a different tactic:

Another commercial, "It's free communication weekend!! Message your matches for free!!"

I thought, "Okay, God. I'll send her an email. It's not going to cost me anything." (Again, I'm picturing a wry smile from God as He knew exactly what this email was going to cost me…my loneliness.)

I don't remember exactly what I said in my first email to Linda. Probably something short and rather lame like, "Hi. I'm Jim. I read your profile and liked it. If you are interested in connecting, let me know. Jim."

I had no idea if this "wonderful on paper" woman would even respond.

But God Knew.

God knew he had been preparing both of us for this exact moment in time. He had heard the prayers, collected the tears, sat right by our side every lonely night, and set His plan in motion many years earlier. We had remained faithful through all the placeholders He put in our lives.

Just a few hours later, while still working on my project, I received an alert that I had mail waiting for me in eHarmony. Hmmm. Well, I thought, at the very least, this woman named Linda has some common courtesy and is probably messaging me to let me know she has found her Ephesians 5 man and is in the exclusive relationship she had been praying for.

Imagine my surprise when I logged back in to read something like, "Hi Jim! It's Linda. Thanks for reaching out. I checked out your profile and I'd like to get to know you better. Would you have time for a phone call today? Linda."

Wait, what? She isn't taken? She wants to talk? I reverted to my reflex fear of "Yes" and my judgmental, "What's wrong with this girl that she isn't taken and wants to talk?" Now what was I going to do?

As it turns out, I couldn't talk that night and I let Linda know that. I already had plans to take Pastor Shoup, his wife, Nancy, and my cousin, Kathy, to see Mannheim Steamroller's Christmas special at the Fox Cities PAC. Linda and I made plans to talk on Tuesday.

More foreshadowing: remember when I told you earlier that who people are in real life is not who they portray themselves to be online and that what you see on social media is not always what you get? Well, you have just read the exception to that rule! The Linda that I know and love in real life is every bit the incredible person she portrayed herself to be online, and more. If you've met her, you know that to be true. You are about to meet Linda and hear the stories of her life, her faith, her family, her friends, and her struggles. Each story is just one piece of an intricate puzzle that shaped her faith, and her, into the person with the qualities you just read about. As you read my story in *God Knew* to get to know me, I encourage you to read Linda's story to get to know her.

God had now set the wheels in motion. Get ready for the ride.

The girl in the red scarf wanted to talk…

CHAPTER 4
ALL BECAUSE TWO PEOPLE
FELL IN LOVE

Mom and Dad, Christmas of 1952

18 Then the LORD God said, "It is not good for the man to be alone. I will make a helper who is just right for him." Genesis 2:18 (NLT)

"And I now pronounce you husband and wife...Jim, you may kiss your bride." Words that, at the initial publishing of his first book in 2015, Jim had given up the hope of ever hearing said to him. I had just about done so, too, at that point in my life. Wait...where are my manners? Allow me to introduce myself...I am the girl in the red scarf... Jim's bride, Linda Meyer, and this is *my God Knew* story.

You will find as you make your way through this book that Jim's and my life stories mirror each other's in many ways, but there are also differences. Jim's family was deeply grounded in the Church for generations and my family's relationship journey with God started small but developed over time. As he mentioned in the original *God Knew*, many of his family members were pastors and his Grandma Meyer taught Christian school. Up until the writing of this manuscript in 2023, no one from my family had been called into the ministry. However, as you continue reading, you will see how my family's Christian legacy began and, as a result, my nephew Tyler just graduated from a Christian university to become a youth minister, and my nephew, Grady will soon begin his sophomore year at a different Christian university studying to be a music minister. What a difference a couple of generations can make.

So, how did a girl from Southeastern Wisconsin end up with a boy from the Northwoods of Wisconsin? Only God knew…He knew exactly which lanes and highways, states, and cities each of our families would traverse that would, ultimately, lead Jim and me to meet each other and to find our happily ever after. But it would take many years and life-building struggles, exercises, and lessons before we would ultimately meet, and our story would begin. Just like Jeremiah 29:11 in the NIV (my life verse) says, *"For I know the plans I have for you, declares the Lord. Plans to prosper you and not to harm you. Plans to give you hope and a future."* But before we get too deep into the present or future, we must understand the past and how God directed our lives and roads to each other. So, buckle up, friends, you're in for quite a ride.

My history began with my parents, Richard and Fritzi Leighton (born Winnifred, but not many dared call her that without getting a stern look, and if you said "Winnie," well, you were in big trouble). My dad was born in Connecticut, and my mom was born in Nebraska, but they both grew up mainly in Madison, Wisconsin. They both were born during and lived through the Great Depression. Due to the hard times those days brought, they both found themselves living in Madison in the 1940s. I don't know a lot of details of their growing-up years, but they shared bits and pieces of their lives over time.

My dad, who went by Dick, and his brother, Philip, were raised mainly by their mom, my beloved Grandma Julie (aka, Grandma Mell), as his parents divorced when they were fairly young. My Grandpa, whom I never had the opportunity to know, would come in and out of their lives, but mostly he was out. He and my grandma did get back together at one point and remarried, only to divorce again after a few years. Grandma worked outside of their home to support them, and Dad had Phil and his other neighborhood friends to play with. They were like most little boys in the '40s, playing cowboys and Indians in the woods (yes, this was a thing in the 1940s) and, after World War II started, they would pretend to be in the military and would fight the "Nazis" together. Dad even tried to hang his brother once like they read about in books (oy vey).

In his early teens, my dad took on a paper route so he could purchase a bike, and also for spending money, but his aspirations quickly turned higher. After only a couple of years of flinging papers, he became the proud owner of his own retired Harley-Davidson police motorcycle. Oh, the joy! It sure made getting up at 4:30 am to deliver the news in the freezing cold temperatures much quicker, and much more fun! This love of motorcycles and cars became one of my dad's major life interests as the years went by.

When it came to church attendance, Grandma did dress the boys up on Sundays and took them to the Lutheran church in their neighborhood. They went regularly, but faith was not talked about much in their family; it was kept very private and was not demonstrative in any way. Church was for Sundays, and the rest of the week was devoted to family, school, and work, and don't forget, there were those "Indians" and "Nazis" to fight…

Across town, my mom grew up with her parents and three sisters, Jo, Trudy, and Nancy. My grandfather, John, had immigrated to the United States from Hungary after World War I in search of a better life. He met and married my grandma, Maude, in Texas and they moved to Nebraska after a few years, where my mom was born. Grandpa was a very strong-willed and opinionated man of German descent who was "always right." Grandma Maude was a very quiet, submissive woman, with an infectious laugh (she also made the best grilled cheese sand-wiches and chocolate chip cookies around). Like my dad's family (and I think most families at that time in history), faith was a part of their up-bringing in the Presbyterian church, but not something that was talked about or lived out other than on Sunday mornings.

So, how did the love story between my parents come about? Well, Dad and Mom met in high school. Similar to how Jim's mom and dad met, my dad was supposed to go out on a date with my aunt Trudy (they played together in the high school band). Then he met my mom, and they hit it off and began dating. My Dad was 17 and Mom was 16. They spent their weekends and summer days riding Dad's Harley on the winding roads up to Baraboo and climbing the bluffs at Devil's Lake State Park or with friends swimming or ice skating at Vilas Park; just enjoying dating and falling in love. It wasn't a perfect love story, though. They would break up a time or two, but eventually got back to-gether and married when Dad was 19 and Mom was 18. Dad joined the Air Force right after and was stationed in Biloxi, Mississippi.

Shortly thereafter, my mom hopped on a train, pregnant and scared, and went to live with Dad on the Air Force base, where he was teaching RADAR school to Air Force cadets during the Korean War. Thankfully, he was never sent overseas, and my two oldest siblings, Sherri and Keith, were born there in Mississippi. Not long after, my dad was honorably discharged from the military for health reasons, so they loaded up their little family and their pup, Dixie, into the car and headed back to Madison, where they lived for a couple of years with my Grandma before moving to Milwaukee. Ultimately, after many years, and with the addition of three more children, Steve, Kathy, and Debbie, they built the family home in Oak Creek, where I was born five years later. My youngest brother, Jim, came into the world 18 months after me. Mom said, "no more" and the doctor performed measures to ensure that there would be no more "surprise blessings" in the future. Seems like my parents took the verses from Psalm 127: 3-5 (NIV) seriously, *"Lo, children are a heritage of the Lord: and the fruit of the womb is his reward. As arrows are in the hand of a mighty man; so are children of the youth. Happy is the man that hath his quiver full of them: they shall not be ashamed...."* I would say, Mom and Dad a quiver-full and another for good measure!

The house was a little three-bedroom ranch with a whole lot of people, but it was a home filled with love ... and a lot of sibling rivalry! Kids being kids, we fought together, but we loved each other. We stuck together and, if someone messed with one of us, they messed with all of us. The questions "what happened?" and "what was that noise?" were quite prevalent in our home. Not to mention "don't make me come out there." I am sure many of you can relate.

As was quite normal in the '60s and '70s, Mom was a home-maker, and Dad was the primary breadwinner. Dad also loved cars and motorcycles, so in order to keep food on the table (and new cars in the garage), he often worked several jobs at a time. Because of that, we kids spent much more time with Mom growing up than we did with Dad. Having said that, he was a good Dad, and he loved us very much.

We didn't have a lot of material things growing up as a family of nine, but we had a lot of love. Mom always did the best she could to make holidays and birthdays special. I have such fond memories of waking up on Valentine's Day with my very own specially created Valentine at my spot at the dinner table and of home-made coffeecake and Easter baskets on Easter morning. I remember crazy Christmas mornings with stockings, and each of us getting a couple of gifts from Mom and Dad, and one from Santa. It was a home filled with a lot of laughter, love, and togetherness.

However, life wasn't always rosy, and it did throw in some pitfalls and difficult times. Several years before I was born, my Grandma Julie fell in love with a wonderful man named Arnie and re-married. They were very happy, but only three years into their marriage, Arnie had a heart attack and passed away. Grandma was devastated and my dad became very angry with God. He felt that it was so unfair that Grandma had lived such a difficult life with his biological father and, after finally finding happiness again, he felt disappointed that God took Arnie away and his Mom was alone again. Because of this, Dad stopped going to church with us as a family and Mom was thrust into being the spiritual leader in our home. She never wavered in wanting her children to grow up with a love for the Lord and made Sunday church attendance a priority. She willingly shouldered the role, and it would soon lead to a complete turnaround to the Christian life for our family in the years to come. She was an amazing mom, and she loved her kids with everything in her.

Mom epitomized the verses from Proverbs 31:30-31 (NIV) that states, *"Charm is deceptive, and beauty is fleeting; but a woman who fears the Lord is to be praised. Honor her for all that her hands have done, and let her works bring her praise at the city gate."*

CHAPTER 5
THE AWAKENING

Revelation 3:20 (NIV) - Here I am! I stand at the door and knock. If anyone hears my voice and opens the door, I will come in and eat with that person, and they with me.

For the first 10 years of my life, we attended Faith Presbyterian Church in Franklin, Wisconsin. I remember very little about my time there, except plunking out "What Child is This" and "Jesus Loves Me" on the old, out-of-tune piano in the fellowship hall while Mom was in choir and of our family attending Easter Sunday sunrise services. My older siblings were part of the youth group, but my younger brother Jim and I were too young for that. My oldest sister, Sherri, and brother Keith each got married within the walls of that church.

But something was missing in my mom's life. She began watching the 700 Club and PTL and, as a child, sometimes I would watch it along with her. Her faith grew strong watching those ministries, as she heard stories about how God worked in people's lives and changed their hearts. She started reading her Bible more and God began changing her heart, too. God was stirring up something in her soul and she was beginning to feel the need for a change. I remember watching one episode of PTL with her, and they were asking for donations, and with any donation amount, you could get a necklace that said, "No Weapon Formed Against Me Shall Prosper." Not that I understood that at my age (I think I was about six or seven), but I asked if I could send in the $1 that I received for my birthday, and they sent that necklace to me in the mail. I found that necklace recently when I was cleaning out our family home and it brought the memory back. That was the start of the child-like faith that became a bedrock in my life as time went on.

In 1979, Billy Graham was set to do a crusade at Milwaukee County Stadium. One day before the crusade, there was a knock at our door. A lovely, godly couple, Don and Joy Wilmot, from Oak Creek Assembly of God (now known as Discover Church) invited Mom to join them at the crusade. Mom decided to attend the crusade, and she took my brother, Jim, along with her. And it was that day that solidified the life change Mom was searching for. As Billy Graham always did, he asked if anyone wanted to ask Jesus into their hearts and surrender their lives to God. Mom followed the call, and she started a new life living for Christ.

After the crusade, we continued attending the Presbyterian church for the early morning service and then raced across town to the Oak Creek Assembly of God church for their 9:30 am service. This only lasted a month or so, and then we transitioned from the Presbyterian church to the Assembly of God church. As you can imagine, it created quite a stir when Mom marched up the center aisle with 6 of her 7 children (and a daughter-in-law) following behind to the very front pew and her tape recorder in hand! The church grew by almost one-tenth that first Sunday! It was there that my family started our new life with God. The most amazing part is that the Pastor that was leading the church at the time, is still the Lead Pastor of the church almost 44 years later!

Our family integrated right in and made many life-long friends. The atmosphere in an Assembly of God church was very different than the Presbyterian Church. The services felt alive to us. We didn't know it at the time, but it was the Holy Spirit moving that we felt. We had never clapped in rhythm to the music or raised our hands in praise to God before this. It was a little bit of an eye-opening experience, but one that just resonated in all our souls. It was during those times that we as a family learned how to worship the Lord openly and with abandon.

Timing-wise, this was during the final years of the "Jesus Revolution" that was birthed in the 1970s. My brother, Steve, was very involved in a Bible study at public school (yes, they used to allow them in those days). There he learned about wonderful Christian artists such as Maranatha, 2nd Chapter of Acts, Keith Green, Phil Keaggy, Love Song, and many others, and brought the records home to share with us. Even to this day, I listen to some of those groups on occasion because their music was so drenched in true worship and had lyrics that just drew hearts into God's presence.

Soon after we began attending the new church, I joined the young girl's group called "Missionettes." It was similar to Girl Scouts but was entirely centered around learning how to be a young lady with godly attributes and ways. My pastor's wife, Sherry, and Mom's new friend Joy, whom I mentioned before, were our leaders. They taught us how to read the Bible, memorize Scriptures, and how to serve others. If we brought our dues, brought a friend, or finished a badge, we got to pick something out of the grab bag. As you can imagine, that was quite an incentive! Sometimes there were full candy bars in there!

We also got to take part in sleep overs and, once a year, we went up to our church's campground in Waupaca, Wisconsin for the annual Missionettes gathering. In all honesty, I did not enjoy spending three nights in a pup tent in early June when it was still chilly outside and there were bugs and other critters that a young tween from the suburbs of southeastern Wisconsin wasn't used to encountering. But I loved the time with my friends and did enjoy creating new adventures during my first real trips away from home at a young age. It's funny now, because still to this day I say that when I'm anywhere near Waupaca, I'm camping, regardless of whether it's in a hotel there or not. This may or may not have been the start of my older sister Debbie beginning to refer to me as a "Princess." But I digress....

After completing the Missionettes Stars program, young ladies got to have their crowning ceremony as an Honor Star at church. My friends, Tammy, Niki, Lisa, and I were the first girls in the history of our church to be crowned. It was a special service. Our fathers got to walk us down the aisle where we received our capes from our moms and our leaders placed a crown on our heads. Incidentally, my mom sewed the capes for us, and those four, along with many others, are still used 40 years later for each new group of Honor Stars that graduate each year. I still have my crown and recently unearthed my Missionettes Handbook while cleaning out the garage at my family home. These were the formative years that just drew me deeper into my relationship with Christ.

After graduating from Missionettes, we moved on to youth group. Our church was growing by leaps and bounds in those years and our youth group became quite large. We had four wonderful youth pastors during my pre-teen and late teen years, and many different youth sponsors, all of whom spoke into our lives the hope and love of Christ and the importance of cultivating and sharing our faith with others. They were each in their own way pivotal mentors to a diverse and energetic group of kids, and we loved them with all our hearts. My youth group friends became my tribe and we had many great adventures at youth camp, youth choir tours, youth conventions, and lock-ins, which brought us closer together and kept us on a road to learning to be more like Jesus. We were challenged not to give in to the pressures and lures that most kids in their teenage years are exposed to. We met regularly on Wednesday evenings but also spent most Friday, Saturday, and Sunday nights (after church) hanging out at restaurants, going bowling, and doing other fun activities. Even now, 40 years later, I have such wonderful and fond memories of our time with each of those youth pastors and friends that resonate in my heart. Two of my youth sponsors, Jeff and Tammi Ratliff, would, in the near future, become like family to me and are now two of my best friends.

There were many joys during these years, but there would also be some hard times. Remember when I mentioned in the previous chapter that my dad was angry at God after the loss of his stepfather? Well, our exciting newfound faith and all the time that we spent at church and in related activities didn't sit well with Dad. He didn't feel a part of it, nor did he want any part of it. It was just too different than what he was used to and the type of church he grew up in. It made him uncomfortable when we talked about God and what He was doing in our lives…something that just didn't happen in his home growing up. He felt church took us away from family time and he wasn't sure he liked that our lives were transforming before his eyes. It caused him to pull away from us and he began doing his own thing on Sundays, riding his motorcycle in summer, or spending time with friends, which ultimately brought heartache and division between my parents.

Even so, it was during those formative years that my faith became very real to me and my relationship with Jesus began to mature. I wanted to live a life that pleased God and, when I was 15 or 16, I made a commitment in my heart and to God to stay sexually pure and wait to share that part of myself with my husband and no other. It seemed like an easy vow to make. Most of my friends were Christians and they all had the same goals and made the same vows I had. And since we mostly hung out together, the temptations were fairly low.

It wasn't strict like that 80's Kevin Bacon movie, *Footloose*, and it's crazy to think about now, but we were taught that dancing could easily lead to bad things and was very much discouraged, so most of us didn't attend school dances or prom. Instead, we'd have creatively fun get-togethers that didn't involve dancing or drinking (well, alcohol that is…remember Jolt soda?) or huge parties while our parents were not home. Instead, we had bonfires and played games, sang songs, and just enjoyed good, wholesome fun. Some of our friends dated each other and we all had our crushes and first kisses but it was all very innocent.

Maybe to some of you, it seems like we had a pretty lame upbringing. Like we missed out on important life events, but we didn't see it that way. We were having fun and staying out of trouble, and it saved most of us from heart ache. You see, I never stumbled home drunk or ever had a pregnancy scare. The police were never called because I had done something bad or that I regretted. I was living a good life and I was thankful for it. But, even still, there were lonely days, too. Friends were great substitutes, but there were days I longed to have a boyfriend like some of my other friends had. Not that there weren't boys I liked or that liked me, but just none that stuck. Deep down, I believe it was because God had other plans for me.

It was during those days that the verses I had memorized in Proverbs 3: 5-6 (NKJV), *"Trust in the Lord with all your heart and lean not on your own understanding; in all your ways acknowledge Him, and He will direct your paths"* became very critical for me to hold in my heart. I would remind myself and stand on them quite often in the future.

As I grew older and transitioned from being a youth group member to being a youth group sponsor, I was still able to do all the fun things that I loved doing as a youth group member, but I also had the opportunity to mentor youth to stay on track with their faith and to help them figure out how to take their walk with God seriously. And it was fun being able to boss them around a bit too.

It was in those days that, due to a devastating circumstance that happened in the youth leadership ministry of our church, I formed a close friendship with Stacey Brooks, who was Pastor Jerry and Sherry Brooks' (the head pastor of our church) daughter. She quickly became one of my best friends and we were inseparable for many years. Because of this, I became very close with her family and spent a lot of time with them. I went to Brooks family reunions and made friends with her cousins. It was at that time I started to see Pastor Jerry and Sherry as my second parents, and I still see them that way some 32 years later. They have been there for me through many ups and downs and never stopped encouraging me in my walk with Christ. Pastor Brooks even jokes that we grew up together, and it's pretty much true.

It was also during this time when my friendship with Jeff and Tammi Ratliff would grow from being a sponsor/youth to being the best of friends and like family. They had married young and went through rough times early on so they would counsel me to enjoy the freedom I had in my early 20s to have fun with friends and to focus on my walk with God; to let God make me into the woman that someone would want to be with and be overjoyed to marry someday. Little did I know how long that wait would be and how many years it would be for this prayer to be answered. But God knew and He is always faithful, and He is always good.

CHAPTER 6
THE LONELY YEARS

"The Lord himself goes before you and will be with you; he will never leave you nor forsake you. Do not be afraid; do not be discouraged."
Deuteronomy 31:8 (NIV)

So, what happened between the time Jeff and Tammi gave me the advice to enjoy the freedom of my single life to when I met Jim? Well, admittedly, those years ended up being pretty lonely at times. And years that brought several major life changes in our family.

It started when my parent's marriage began to deteriorate. Initially, it was them watching TV in separate rooms with a lot of yelling out to each other from room to room, then escalating to their one bedroom becoming two. I was still living at home at the time, and the atmosphere became tense, to say the least. There was no fighting; my dad didn't fight. Mom may have wanted to have her say, but Dad would just shut down when discussions became heated.

Around the same time, my mom's health issues intensified. She had lived with arthritis in her legs and her back for a long time, but now walking and getting around was more difficult. She had a tough time making meals and doing the household chores, which put further stress on their marriage.

Then, in 1995, just 3 days after my 25th birthday, I received a call at work from my sister Debbie. Dad was moving out. He was unhappy and just felt like he couldn't live in our home anymore. He had found an apartment a couple of miles away and he went to live on his own. The heart of the little girl who used to snuggle with her Daddy in his chair before bed, waiting for the tickles that were sure to come, broke wide open. Because for me, he didn't just leave Mom...he left me, too.

Perhaps that might sound a little dramatic, but feelings are feelings. I had moved from being single and carefree, without much responsibility, to being thrust into the world of caregiver to my mom. I was working full time and now taking care of Mom. I had become the woman of the house, as well, with all the activities and tasks that entailed (cleaning, making meals, grocery shopping) and all the while trying to not get angry and bitter at being placed in this position. I'd like to tell you that I rose above those feelings and pulled myself up by my bootstraps and just soldiered on, and some days I did. But in my low moments, I did wallow a bit. I felt sad and afraid that I was stuck in a life that didn't belong to me and time was quickly passing me by.

You may be wondering, though, why I haven't mentioned my parents divorcing. Well, because they never did. They never lived together again, but they stayed married for the rest of their lives. Although it was hard and hurtful when Dad left, he still provided for my mom and did what he could to take care of her. He came over every weekday to get Mom lunch so that she was able to stay in the family home, and to stay connected with each other and what was going on in the family. Crazy right? Well, it ended up being how they worked through things and because of that, we could meet for holidays and birthdays without angst or heightened tensions.

Not long after my dad left, one of my brothers got married and, in the next 4 years, another brother and two sisters got divorced. What in the world, right?? Satan was obviously very afraid of what God had planned for our family because he sure did his darndest to tear our family apart.

So, in all this, how did I handle my emotions? Well, I got angry and frustrated and cried a lot. I often felt sorry for myself and I ate a lot of brownies. And, I bought more shoes than a girl could wear out in 7 lifetimes (because shoes still fit even when your largest size jeans didn't, right?).

My favorite was when well-meaning (I think) acquaintances would ask me why I was still single. "You're such a catch," they'd say. "What are the guys you meet thinking?" I'd like to say I always answered them with grace, responding that it just wasn't God's timing for me yet to find someone, but that wasn't always true. Sometimes the sarcastic, frustrated words would come out, like "Well, I can't imagine why, since the line is so long, and I've been beating them off with sticks!"

Is there anyone else that has felt that way or had someone say those words to you? What seemed like a back-handed compliment instead hurt you because you had felt and thought those same things, and you couldn't understand what was wrong with you. If that has happened to you, just know that you are not alone. I think those people who said that really are well-intentioned and truly meant to say those words to encourage you, but it can come off as painful when you've been asking yourself those questions. Having said that, I never for a minute felt that God forgot about me. There were times that I was honest enough to think that He was taking His sweet time moving me from my current circumstances into a life of my own, but I always trusted His will and His plans for me.

So, what did I do in the meantime? Like any self-respecting girl would do, I became a mommy to several dogs and a cat (not at the same time, but over a span of close to 30 years I had three dogs and one cat—I used to say that my cat himself had three dogs). I had pets to meet that need to mother. I knew I didn't need to have a man in my life to make this happen—I could be a fur mommy all on my own. They were my babies that had fur and paws instead of soft pink skin and I loved them like I would any baby that would ever come from me. I went full "Sarah" from the book of Genesis and took matters into my own hands to fill the void I was feeling. But the difference is, fur babies don't live all that long, and you have to say goodbye way sooner than you are ever ready to.

I'd like to say that I didn't continue to self-medicate during those days by buying way too many pairs of shoes, but I will say that I wasn't angry with God. In hindsight, the mistake I did make was not always turning to Him to pour out my soul, or to seek the comfort that I needed from the only One that truly could give me comfort. Although I never lost hope that He would get me through these struggles, and I never doubted His love for me or that He had good plans for me and my life, I also didn't always ask for His help to change me even if my circumstances didn't change. I did not understand that He was using this time of waiting to build my character and turn me into the woman of God that He always intended for me to be.

Fast forward another five years. On a cold day in early March of 2005, my brother Keith passed away suddenly from a heart attack and our family was, again, thrown into another layer of grief and loss. While my mom had the certainty that my brother was with Jesus, my dad wasn't quite able to take comfort in that. Pastor Brooks gave an amazing sermon at Keith's funeral, and, in a true understanding of God's wisdom, he stated that we could all say goodbye to Keith at that moment, or we could say see you later—it was up to us. He then gave our family an opportunity to ask Jesus in our hearts and my dad accepted Jesus back into his heart that day. He knew then and there that he had to make that choice to open his heart to Jesus, or possibly live with the reality that he might not be with his family in heaven when that day came. His life didn't miraculously change at that point, and he never did attend church regularly, but over time his anger at God began to dissipate.

By 2008, my mom's health had gone downhill enough to where we had to make the difficult decision to move her from the family home to a nursing home. Her muscles had atrophied to the point that she was no longer able to walk. Since I had taken care of her for so many years (13 years at that point), it was decided that I would be her power of attorney for both health and financial matters. Within a few days, we had her settled into a nursing home. And because I can't make this stuff up, at the very same time, my dad was going through a health scare of his own. His heart was in A-fib and needed to be restarted through a cardiac ablation. He was also diagnosed with an ulcer and needed to have an endoscopy to cauterize and treat the ulcer.

Oh, and did I mention that I had a trip scheduled to Disney World that same week as all this was happening? Well, I may not have mentioned it, but it was true. So, my sisters had to step in to help my dad through his health issues and help Mom get settled into the nursing home while I got some very much-needed time away in the happiest place on Earth with my brother Steve and his family. We had a fun time together, but I spent much of the time checking in on Mom and Dad. As much as I wanted to rest, relax, and rejuvenate, it was hard knowing what my parents were going through. I had spent so much time in the caregiving role at that point that I didn't know how to take a step back and enjoy time for myself.

Within the next several weeks, Mom was settled into the nursing home, and the decision was made for Dad to come back to live at the family home, where I was still living. I moved from caregiving for my mom to now watching over my dad and his health. It was different than with Mom, though. His overall health was such that he could take care of himself and could come and go as he pleased. I was in my late thirties, and I felt like a huge weight of responsibility had just been lifted. I could breathe again.

Enter Proverbs 31 Ministries Online Bible Studies on stage right.

CHAPTER 7
JOY COMES IN THE MOURNING

"In his favor is life: weeping may endure for a night, but joy cometh in the morning." Psalm 30:5b (KJV)

How do we deal with times of mourning and devastating loss in our lives? Isn't that one of those questions that just doesn't have a right answer? God chooses to help each of us work through these types of situations in our lives differently. He knew just who I would need to walk with and beside me through those sad, dark days of loss to come.

It's not like I didn't know that my parents wouldn't live forever, and that life has high peaks and low valleys, but I don't feel like any of us are ever ready to face those days when they come our way. It's important for us to keep our eyes on Jesus because He will help us through them. Perhaps one of the most famous of the Psalms...Psalms 23:4 (NIV), says, *"Even though I walk through the darkest valley, I will fear no evil, for you are with me; your rod and your staff, they comfort me."* Those were comforting words that I would cling to for dear life in the ensuing years.

Proverbs 31 Ministries

In January of 2011, I was listening to K-LOVE on the radio, and I heard an interview with Lysa TerKeurst, the president of Proverbs 31 Ministries. She was talking about a new book she had written that centered around learning to crave God more than food, shopping...whatever thing that you put first before God in your life. I had heard spots on the radio periodically for Proverbs 31, but I hadn't really looked into that organization up until that point. However, that day, after hearing Lysa's interview, I went to their website and saw that they were starting a brand-new concept—an online Bible study—for women who wanted to study the Bible with other women but just didn't have time in their lives to meet in-person.

Because I was working quite a bit of overtime at my job at the time and was also at a place where I felt I was too old for the singles group and too young for the adult Bible study class, I decided to join the very first Proverbs 31 Online Bible Study, or "OBS" for short. The study was led by a sweet lady named Melissa Taylor, who was a busy mom with four kids. She was looking for a group of women to study with using her personal blog. She prayed that maybe 50 people would sign up, and boy was she surprised when that 50 turned into 2,500!

I loved the content we were studying, and I was learning how important digging in and studying the Bible was to boost our faith. What I could not have known at that time was the joy I would find, the friendships I would build, and the impact that that one decision to become part of this ministry would make in my life. I had been in a lonely place for a long time and becoming part of this amazing group of women began to awaken me from my slumber and loneliness to really live again. God was doing a new thing in me, and I was flourishing in my faith.

In 2012, I became a volunteer with Proverbs 31 and OBS, and I would work with and under many amazing women who just wanted to serve and help to eradicate Biblical poverty throughout the world. My leadership skills grew under their encouragement and a dream started to build in me. I knew just how much my life had been impacted by this amazing ministry, and I wanted to use what I learned and the joy that had grown in me to reach other women that were just like me; those who felt that maybe life was just passing them by or who had just lost hope of ever being used by God and making an impact in this world. I knew that God was birthing in me a gift of encouragement; I just wasn't sure how He would use me to share it.

I had joined Facebook several years earlier but mainly used it as a place to tell funny stories about my life and to share those funny little memes that started popping up (did we ever think those would catch on so big?). Then, I purposely started following the pages of women with strong faith like Joyce Meyer, Christine Caine, Ann Voskamp, Jennie Allen, Lysa TerKeurst, Angie Smith, and godly men like Steven Furtick, Louis Giglio, Craig Groeschel, and Max Lucado. When I saw something that encouraged me, I started sharing those posts on my different social media platforms figuring that if it encouraged me, others might benefit from reading them, too. I began to see numerous comments from friends and family members on those posts and received messages asking me to continue sharing them because they were blessed and inspired by my doing so. Because of that encouragement, my dream of encouraging and ministering to others began to take shape.

Unfortunately, as usually happens when something big and good starts to be birthed, the enemy comes in to try to steal, discourage, and destroy. You see, just at the same time, my mom's health began to decline exponentially. It started with medication issues that caused her to hallucinate and experience things that weren't there, and there was an initial diagnosis of dementia. But I never believed that diagnosis because her brain could still be so sharp. I just knew in my heart it was something else. So, I began researching the different medications she was taking and worked with a pharmacist to determine that it was very likely that certain medications were interacting negatively, causing her to hallucinate and become confused and fearful. To help her from being afraid, I printed out Bible verses about how she didn't have to fear because God had redeemed her and she was His—that was her favorite one—and others about how God had plans for her, to give her hope and a future. I taped them up all over her room and she would read them, and even in her confusion, it brought her comfort and peace.

Being her medical power of attorney did help in this situation because I was able to get her moved temporarily to a drug and substance treatment center and, as I thought, the staff there determined it was medication related. As such, they removed her from all the medications she had been taking, and, lo and behold, she began to come out of the fog she had been living under! It took several months, but I began to get my mom back.

It was during that time she prayed and asked God how He could use her there in the nursing home to impact the people there. God showed her that she might not be able to get out of bed, but she could pray. She started praying with the nurses and aides. They would sit with her in the evenings because they felt drawn to her because of her faith, and they were grateful for her prayers. She also prayed for her family like never before. She would tell me often that she was praying for God to bring the perfect godly man into my life that would share my faith and become my soulmate. She prayed that God would use us as a couple someday to make an impact for His kingdom. It meant so much to me to know that my beloved mom wanted to make sure that I would be loved and taken care of after she was gone from this world.

In 2012, Mom was diagnosed with congestive heart failure and COPD. She was placed on high levels of oxygen and began to really struggle to breathe. She was rushed to the hospital several times over the next year and finally in September of 2013, her legs were eternally healed, and she walked into the arms of Jesus. As you can imagine, after being her primary caregiver for 18 years, my heart was broken. While I was so thankful that she was no longer suffering or in pain, I had lost my Mama and I was hurting.

It was then that my new friends from Proverbs 31 circled the wagons and loved on me like I had never experienced before. They left their phones on overnight just in case I would need someone to talk to or pray with and checked in on me often. My best friend, Tammi, was living in Florida and she also checked in on me almost daily during that time. These friends exemplified the love of Jesus and really helped me through those very difficult days. In fact, just a month after Mom passed, Tammi and I met in Florida and went on a cruise with my friends from Proverbs 31. It was a time of healing with those cherished friends.

As I continued to volunteer with Proverbs 31, it was determined that it was high time that all of us girls got together for an OBS reunion! So, in September of 2014, a group of about 100 of us all met up in Asheville, North Carolina at The Billy Graham Training Center at the Cove. It was in a gorgeous setting and it was so amazing to finally meet in person the women who had been so impactful in my walk with God over those last several years. There were many hugs and tears, great times of laughter, and just enjoying the beauty of God's creation in the Appalachian Mountains. We had wonderful times of worship, listened to the different leaders share their stories, took part in breakout sessions, and spent time at the altar seeking God, asking Him to show us how He planned to use us for His Kingdom in the coming years.

In one of the evening meetings, my friend Nicki Koziarz stepped off the stage and made a beeline for me. She said that God shared with her that He saw me, saw the things I had done for Him, and was pleased. He wanted me to know that He wanted to use me to change generations! Here's that note from my journal:

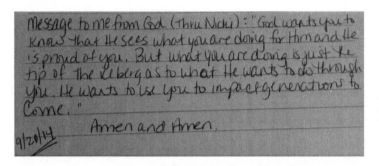

As you can imagine, I was undone. I made my way down to the altar and asked my friend Lisa Allen to pray for me for God's direction, and the message Nicki had just shared with me. She asked me how I thought God wanted to use me: would it be through speaking, writing, or something else? I told her I didn't know for sure yet, but I knew that God had called me all those years ago to speak into the lives of women and to share God's goodness to encourage them. At that time, I could not have known that less than 9 years later, I would be sitting at my computer writing the words of my story to be part of a book called, *God Knew, Faithfulness Fulfilled*! How awesome is that?? God is so good!

Also, during that trip, I had the opportunity to visit the Billy Graham Museum in Charlotte, North Carolina. It's a big, barn-like structure with a giant cross window above the entry. When you first step in, they have a little area to watch some old-time movies showing the different crusades that Billy Graham did all over the world. I imagined that one of those depicted on the screen was at Milwaukee County Stadium and that my mom and brother were sitting in the audience there. As I shared earlier in this book, it was at one of Billy's crusades that my mom gave her heart and life to Jesus and now here I was, thirty years later, visiting the place that memorialized Billy's life. It was so humbling to see and be reminded of how his ministry had brought me to where I was in life that day, and I felt like life had come full circle. Because God knew.

The amazing ladies who volunteered with the Proverbs 31 Online Bible Studies at our retreat in 2014.

I truly believe with all my heart that God brought me to Proverbs 31 Ministries and OBS when He did because He knew that if I didn't have the renewed faith and the support of godly women around me, I would really struggle when my mom passed from this life. Some of you may understand this because when you are a caregiver for a long period of time, it becomes part of your identity. When the person you were caring for is no longer there, it's very hard to find your place. There's a lot of time to fill, and you must be careful to fill it with the right things, so you don't spiral into depression or worse. Thankfully, I clung to Jesus and my friends, and my heart was comforted.

The Hearties

It was also just shortly after Mom passed, while watching Hallmark Christmas movies with my dad and sister Kathy, I saw the first commercials for a new original series that Hallmark was releasing called "When Calls the Heart." It was the story of a wealthy, naïve, first-time schoolteacher who took a position in a small town in the Northeast Territory whose students had all lost their fathers in a coal mine accident. At the same time, a handsome Canadian Mountie was assigned to work in that same town, ostensibly at the request of the teacher's father to keep his daughter safe.

It was just the sort of show that Mom would have loved, and I knew we would have watched it together. The antics and witty banter that ensued between the teacher and the Mountie brought laughter and joy to my heart and continued the process of healing. That little show became widely popular and social media pages were started; and a grass-roots army of women (and to the surprise of many, men as well) was born. They would lovingly be called "The Hearties" by the writers and producers of that successful show. I began interacting with the other members of the groups via social media and found another whole community of people who loved the show just as much as I did. They all had stories of why the show resonated with them or why it brought them joy. Through my interactions with them, little by little, my heart stopped hurting as much, and happiness and laughter were more prevalent in my life again. I had found something wholesome and innocent to fill the space the loss of my mom had opened.

I would remember Mom's prayer that I would find love with a wonderful man, and I realized I wanted it. Wasn't this just the perfect time for me to begin praying for him and waiting on God to bring me the one HE had planned for me? But how and where to find said "perfect" man? That's the age-old question. And one that would not be easily answered in the months ahead. But God knew the answer.

CHAPTER 8
WAIT GAIN: A WOMAN'S PERSPECTIVE

"³Not only that, but we rejoice in our sufferings, knowing that suffering produces endurance, ⁴and endurance produces character, and character produces hope, ⁵and hope does not put us to shame, because God's love has been poured into our hearts through the Holy Spirit who has been given to us." Romans 5:3-5 (ESV)

Weight gain. Definitely not words that any woman of any age ever wants to talk about or experience. Sadly, I've walked that road, too, for most of my life. But this chapter isn't about that kind of weight. This chapter is about waiting to gain. Waiting for the best thing instead of something just okay or that's just good enough. It's about what we gain by waiting on God for His best and not giving in to the pressures of society to settle for what might be adequate. But, instead, allow God to lead you to His BEST choice for you.

The Waiting Game

Sounds pretty easy right? God knows everything—He knows the end from the beginning, so He already chose, out of all the men currently living in this world, who would be your soulmate and your happily ever after. I mean, He knows, right? God knows you, so He knows your hopes and dreams. He knows how lonely you are and that you have longed for your whole life to be a mom to five kids someday. How you have longed to experience what it feels like to carry children inside of you and to give birth to them; to raise them to be sons and daughters of God, just like your mom did with you and your brothers and sisters.

He was with you when you donned bridesmaid dress after bridesmaid dress and bought gifts for countless bridal showers and weddings; and then He watched as, over and over again, you walked up to the kiosk at Target to print out the baby registry for the baby shower you were attending (and truly rejoicing with) as most every one of those friends whose weddings you participated in became mommies.

He knows that biological clocks tick, quietly at first and then get louder and louder like clanging cymbals and that there are only so many ticks of that watch before the dream of having said kids slowly begins to fade away, and until it becomes just a dream you once had.

It's likely obvious that the "you" in the above scenario was me and those were all thoughts that swirled around my mind for many years. I was genuinely happy to celebrate the joy of every one of those occasions, but the belief that those celebrations would ever happen for me began to fade as each year passed and the waiting continued.

During that season in my life, even though I was desiring a relationship and a family, I still had a longing in my heart to know God and understand Him more, too. I sought out sermons and messages that would help me in my everyday life and my relationship with God. For years I had often watched messages from Elevation Church, and Pastor Steven Furtick. Back in 2011, he preached a sermon series called "Mr. and Mrs. Betterhalf" and one of the messages in the series really stuck in my mind and heart.

This specific sermon was directed toward those who hadn't yet found his or her better half. His focus was on the story in Genesis 24 of Abraham asking his servant to find a wife for his son Isaac, but not in the land of Canaan—meaning, not in a land outside of God's will. He reminded us of God's promise to Abraham in the Bible that he would become the father of many nations. He emphasized that we must take those promises from God's Word and meditate on them and pray them back to Him because the Word of God never returns void. And in our waiting, Pastor Steven reminded us that instead of dwelling so much on hearing the four words "Will you marry me," we should instead focus on the four words, "God has promised me." So, when life got tough and the days of waiting grew long, we could remind Him, and stand on these words: "But God You promised." There are many great insights for a single believer in this message. To save yourself heartache, I would highly suggest you listen to it and let the message get deep in your heart, then replay it as often as needed to keep the encouragement alive. (The full message can be found here: https://elevationchurch.org/sermons/an-arranged-marriage [1]).

---

[1] Property of Elevation Church. As of the time of this writing, the link above was active.

I prayed those words that day, and many times thereafter. I listened to that sermon many times for several years, reinforcing the message in my mind and heart. I hid that promise in the back of my mind and believed that I was trusting and waiting for God to move, truly believing I might not see the answer to my prayer yet, but God might still have sent the answer. If I prayed and entrusted it to the Lord, He was moving to answer that prayer.

But, because God knew how my story would end, and that the way He wanted to answer that prayer was bigger than I could ever hope to imagine, He still needed to do a work in me and in my heart. I needed to truly understand that He is not a genie in a lamp, and if I just rubbed the lamp, He would come out and give me three wishes and do my bidding. He wanted me to truly trust that He is the God of the universe, and that my times were in His hands.

Therefore, He allowed me to walk a longer road in order for me to gain insight and maturity along the way. He wanted me to get to know Him more intimately; to hide His Word in my heart deeply to keep me from sin. Ultimately, His answer for me at that point in my life was "not yet." He knew that even though I had the desire to be in a relationship, I wasn't quite emotionally or spiritually ready, and there are things that He wanted to teach me through the circumstances that would come my way.

Sadly, instead of continuing to fully stand on God's promises, I would follow in Sarah's footsteps from Genesis yet again, and I would begin to slowly take matters into my own hands.

The Dating Game

As I said at the end of chapter five, "little did I know how long that wait would be and how many years it would be before this prayer was answered." Thankfully, I wasn't 80-some years old at this time, like Sarah was, but there was a restlessness in me that thought I might just help God along a bit. I mentioned that at the age of 16, I had made the commitment to God to stay pure until marriage and doing so at that time didn't seem like such a stretch, for surely it wouldn't be super long before I would meet "the one" and we'd marry and begin our lives together. I can tell you for absolute certainty that never in my wildest dreams would I have thought that I would make it up into my 40s and still be a virgin, with no prospects and no idea when that might change.

So, I decided…well, to be more truthful, my friend decided… it was time for me to jump headlong into the pool (and sadly often a cesspool) of online dating. And I use that word "dating" loosely, because, if any of you had the same experience as I did, it wasn't as much dating as it was texting or, if you are lucky, talking on the phone. The text and/or phone discussions would start out innocently enough, but then, inevitably, the questions would come about my previous dating life and whether I had been married before, and what my dating experience was. Because I always wanted to be honest, I would share that I had never been married, and I didn't have much experience to speak of due to the decisions I had made to take care of my mom. The responses were almost always ones of unbelief, and in most cases, a turnoff. They would say that it was just not normal for someone at my age to not be sexually active. When they heard that I was still living in our family home, regardless that I was watching over my dad, I was almost always ghosted after that.

And that's when the enemy would come in and try to make me feel like a loser and that something was wrong with me. In my lowest moments, I'll be honest that those words would begin to swirl around in my mind, and I would forget my *but God You promised* prayer. I'd be tempted to just go to a bar, pick someone up and just sleep with them to get it over with so I could lose the stigma of being the 40ish-year-old virgin. Because, weirdly enough, it seemed like many of the men I talked with had the mindset that they would rather be with someone experienced than someone who was untouched. How backward is that?

I'm not proud of having those thoughts, or even for a moment that I considered doing something so against God's Word and plan for me, but they were there just the same. Praise be to God that I never acted upon those thoughts. I'm not saying that I didn't make mistakes along the way and that there wasn't kissing and touching that went outside of the boundaries, but I'm thankful that it never went past the point of no return. I still saved the ultimate act of intimacy for my future husband.

I knew it is a gift that you can't ungive and I wanted to keep that vow I made to God so long ago.

Thankfully, because I know God was still with me and He knew the plans He had for me, there was one guy I was messaging with who had a conscience (and enough of a sense of decency) to tell me to get off the dating sites because they weren't right for me. He knew that, although there are exceptions, in my two and a half years of experience, the majority of those who are on those sites are on there to hook up or for other nefarious reasons, like leading you on and then asking for money (yes, that truly did happen, and no, I did not give him any). But it was then that God, through that one guy, reminded me that even if I couldn't see it at that point because I had believed a lie and felt the rejection so often, I was indeed a daughter of the King and I was meant for more. I was precious in His sight and a pearl of great price. I had temporarily forgotten that.

The Roadblocks

So, I took a step back, repented of my sins, asked forgiveness for taking things into my own hands and my resulting actions, thanked God for His protection, and deleted all the dating apps. I began to focus more on my relationship with God and spending time with friends. I got even more involved in the music ministry at Discover Church. I dug into books about following God's plan for my life and what that might look like. I even considered moving to North Carolina to be closer to my Proverbs 31 friends (and maybe inquiring about a job with them), and attending Elevation Church, which had many campuses in that area. I had visited there once on vacation, and it seemed like a church where I would really fit in. It seemed like a church where I could begin serving, and maybe…just maybe, meet someone there. I would be in a different environment and in a state where no one knew me – I could make a fresh start! However, I wanted to lay my will down and let God's will be done. Because He knew what His plans were for me, another roadblock was set up in my path. And the wait for His perfect timing would continue.

In the spring of 2016, my dad was diagnosed with stage 3 prostate cancer; so instead of moving to another state, I would take on the role of caregiver again.

Dad would begin undergoing chemotherapy treatments at the beginning of June of that year. One hot Saturday morning after his first chemo treatment, my dad decided to take my dog for a walk. Thankfully he always followed the same route, because while walking, he became very dizzy and passed out in the street. By God's grace, someone saw him right away and called 911. As you can imagine, my dog was extremely distraught. She didn't want anyone to go near my dad and even tried to bite the policeman who tried to put her into his car to bring her home. Thankfully, a neighbor who was a nurse rode up to the scene on his bike, brought her home, and alerted me of the situation. Because God is a God of providence, during that walk Dad's blood pressure dropped to a very low 60/40 which caused him to pass out. Had that not happened and he hadn't been taken directly to a nearby hospital, we might never have realized that he had developed a dangerous saddle clot over the top of both of his lungs from the chemotherapy. He spent several days in the ICU and was released several days later having been placed on blood thinners. Unfortunately, just a few days later he started feeling very ill again, and we had to take him to the VA hospital in our area. There it was determined that he had a serious blood infection. He would need someone to watch over him to help with his treatments and to make sure he didn't fall again or cut himself while on the blood thinners. So, I put my plans/dreams to move to North Carolina on the back burner and chose to stay and watch over Dad and help him. He underwent treatment for about a year, and praise God, his cancer was cured. Dad went into remission in early 2017.

The Wait Gain

Through it all, God was always good. The verses in Romans 5:3-5 that I quoted at the beginning of this chapter had proven to be true in my life and they can be in your life, too. Although I can honestly say I didn't always rejoice in my sufferings and all the waiting, my character was definitely shaped by all of the rejection that I had encountered and the trials that I had faced over my life, but there were also often rays of hope. And I learned the lesson that God was teaching me…He can be trusted, even when we can't see if things are happening or not.

I knew walking along this wait-gain road that I needed to acknowledge that my ways are not God's ways, my timing is not always His timing, and trying to "manage" my life often caused delays instead of progress. I believe I had to walk through another "not yet" season, standing on the promise that God's Word is true. I had to have the faith to stand with Him and believe it. The words in 2 Corinthians 1:20 (NLT), *"For all of God's promises have been fulfilled in Christ with a resounding 'Yes!' And through Christ, our 'Amen' (which means 'Yes') ascends to God for his glory,"* can be trusted.

Friends, if you find that you are in a time of "not yet" or "no," I beg you to not get angry at God or give up hope. I know that might sound super easy for me to say…now. But I am a living, breathing, example that God's promises are true, and He does know our hearts and longs to be your first love. If you have never thought much about God or opening your heart to Him, I would say to you now, DO IT! Read His Word and get to know who He is intimately. Hebrews 4:12 (NLT) says, *"For the word of God is alive and powerful. It is sharper than the sharpest two-edged sword, cutting between soul and spirit, between joint and marrow. It exposes our innermost thoughts and desires."* He knows what you are thinking and feeling at every moment. He knows your hurts and pain and loneliness. And He wants to hold you through it all.

You absolutely cannot know for certain where God is going to lead you in this life on earth. But I also know in my heart that, regardless of your circumstances, God is sovereign, and He is faithful. He is good and His plans for your life are good, and they are plans to prosper you (and this doesn't always mean monetarily) and to give you hope and a future.

Psalm 56:8 (NLT) states, *"You keep track of all my sorrows. You have collected all my tears in your bottle. You have recorded each one in your book."* You may never have heard that before and are wondering how that can be true because you feel so abandoned and alone. But that verse right there shows you that He sees you. He made you in His image – and you are not alone.

For me, through all my trials and struggles, I never doubted His goodness or His love for me, but that doesn't mean I didn't get discouraged. Of course, I did; I am human. But in hindsight, I can now see that all the roadblocks I had encountered were God's protection and for me to grow and mature in Him. He wanted me to learn through my dating circumstances that doing it my way and taking things into my own hands is not the road He wanted for me. Proverbs 16:9 (NIV) says, *"In their hearts humans plan their course, but the Lord establishes their steps."* And, because I had waited decades for His promises to be fulfilled and had finally surrendered my will into His most capable hands, the wait would soon be over. The wait had finally produced the gain.

And the Sunday morning of Thanksgiving weekend 2017, God answered my *but God You promised* prayer and He sent my prince.

CHAPTER 9
TO DREAM THE "IMPOSSIBLE"...LIST?

"When you have eliminated the impossible, whatever remains, however improbable, must be the truth." – Sir Arthur Conan Doyle, stated by Sherlock Holmes

"Jesus looked at them and said, 'With man this is impossible, but with God all things are possible'" – Matthew 19:26 (ESV)

In a previous chapter, I referenced an Excel spreadsheet list I created that contained all the must-haves, needs, and wants for my future wife. It's sort of an impossible list when you think about it. As Pastor Shoup laughed, and then chided me when I showed him this list, "Sixty-seven qualities!! 67 qualities? Jim, most people would be happy with five really good qualities, but 67? C'mon!"

Linda has just shared with you who she is, and you've gotten to know my wife and most of her exceptional qualities and characteristics.

As it turns out, I did not find, and God did not provide, a woman that fulfilled all 67 things. But what would you give the odds of finding a woman that fulfilled even half (33) of those things? How about a woman that fulfilled one-quarter (16) of those things? Pretty skinny odds on the probability of either of those happening, right? How about even finding a woman with the five that Pastor Shoup talked about?

Now I don't have a degree in statistics, and I don't gamble so I don't know how they calculate the odds of something happening. But my gut intuition tells me that the odds of a woman having 65 of the 67 characteristics on my list is pretty infinitesimal, almost approaching the impossible.

If that is indeed the case, I guess you could also refer to Linda as my "impossible" dream come true!

For those of you who think, "You know, having some sort of list might not be a bad idea. I wonder what sort of things I'd put on that list?" please allow me to share my list with you. Again, this is my list so I can have things on here that don't necessarily make sense to anybody else, but they are/were important to me.

	M/N/W	Characteristic
	M=Must have (deal breakers), N=Need (might not be a deal breaker,	
	but it's more than a Want), W=Want (nice to have)	
1	M	Christian (preferably LCMS or WELS Lutheran)
2	M	Strong, open faith in Jesus/God/Trinity
3	M	Bible study (church & personal) each week (but also read some Bible verses every day)
4	M	Prays daily
5	M	Worships every week (preferably with me)
6	M	Soulmate/Best Friend - Loves me unconditionally and forever ("in love" with me and desires me, not just "loves" me)
7	M	Believes in 100%/100%/100% in a relationship (not 50/50)
8	M	The "IT" factor (can't explain - just know)
9	M	Faithful & Honest (to me, especially, but also to those she loves)
10	M	Authentic/genuine/down to earth
11	M	Non-smoker
12	M	Pastor Shoup approval
13	N	Strong family values and connections
14	N	Good group of close friends with strong connections
15	N	Has a great deal of common sense
16	N	Stewardship - Charitable with Time/Talents/Treasures (okay to tithe)
17	N	Community minded-will volunteer with me
18	N	Wants to help me expand "God Knew" ministry
19	N	Gets along with my family (even though sometimes I don't)

20	N	Gets along with my best friends
21	N	Good conversationalist/articulate/good communicator
22	N	Good sense of humor (can even be dry and a little sarcastic, but not mean or raw)
23	N	Social skills (can attend community events with me)
24	N	Kind/thoughtful - appreciates little things
25	N	Happy disposition - nice laugh
26	N	Affectionate - PDA is okay (holding hands, etc.)
27	N	Encouraging, but not pushy
28	N	Social drinker (no bar flys)
29	N	Nice voice
30	N	Pretty smile (smiles a lot)
31	N	Hygienic
32	N	Great kisser
33	N	Great hugger
34	N	Great cuddler/snuggler
35	N	No criminal record
36	N	Financially responsible
37	N	Likes to have fun (road trips, concerts, picnics, movies (in or out), dinners, etc.)
38	N	Willing to wait until marriage for sex
39	N	Has my back (as I will have hers)
40	N	I get along with her family and friends
41	N	Conservative political beliefs (not right-wing, though)
42	N	Pro-Life
43	N	Would support me working in church ministry (literally and figuratively)
44	N	LOVES Christmas (decorating (inside and outside), baking, caroling, family & friends, Christmas Eve Candlelight Service, Christmas lights tour with hot chocolate, giving extra to charity, etc.)
45	N	Does NOT play games in the relationship
46	W	Open with emotions, but not in a bad way
47	W	Likes to cook and bake (and eat)
48	W	Green Bay Packers fan (die-hard)

49	W	Educated
50	W	Happy with career choice
51	W	Would be willing to relocate for me, if needed
52	W	Makes me want to be a better person
53	W	Analytical, planner, but also spontaneous
54	W	Healthy (ish)
55	W	Lives a fairly healthy lifestyle with diet & exercise (to help support my health goals)
56	W	Low maintenance
57	W	Plays golf
58	W	Plays tennis
59	W	Likes walking/hiking
60	W	Likes to fish
61	W	Between 5'6"-5'10"
62	W	Age 45-53
63	W	No children or older children
64	W	Would go on a mission trip with me someday
65	W	Competitive, but is neither a sore loser nor poor winner (unless in good fun)
66	W	Can rock a baseball cap and ponytail while casual
67	W	Good driver; willing to drive us to certain events/trips

Friends, that is a 97% score. Sixty-five of sixty-seven things (okay, true confessions: the raw number is 64. However, for golfing and fishing, Linda said she wouldn't do those activities but would go along and read a book while I golf and fish. I gave her a half-point for each one).

I'd like to take a moment and comment on just a couple of the qualities on my list:

- Qualities 1-5: A good relationship, and ultimately a great marriage, takes more than just the two of you. You need to have Jesus/God as the third and most important strand in your marriage (that's the 100/100/100 you see). You will notice my first five "must haves" deal with her faith. And not just with her faith, but in how she lives out her faith on a daily and weekly basis. James 2:14 (ESV) says, *"What good is it, my brothers, if someone says he has faith but does not have works? Can that faith save him?"*

- Qualities 13, 14, 19, 20, and 40: Let's face it, when you marry someone, you are going to have a relationship with their family, and their friends. For almost the first four months of our dating life, we rarely had an "alone date" because we were constantly introducing each other to our family and friends. Linda and I took that even one step further: Pastor Shoup is one of my best friends, and I greatly respect his judgment. Hence, his approval was a "must-have" (#12). Pastor Jerry Brooks at Discover Church in Oak Creek is like a second dad to Linda. She wanted Pastor Brooks' approval of me because she values and respects his judgment. In fact, as you will read in another chapter, I not only asked Linda's biological dad for his blessing before I asked Linda to marry me, but I also asked Pastor Brooks for his permission. If you have those special people in your life, and you find yourself interested in someone, don't be afraid to ask them to be a barometer for you.

- Get to know each other's "Five Love Languages" early on. There is an assessment you can take. Linda and I did this well after I had created this list, and we are amazingly similar. Comparing my list above to those five love languages reveals: physical touch (26, 31, 32, 33, 34, and 38), words of affirmation (9, 10, 21, 22, 23, 25, 27, 45, 46), acts of service (16, 17, 18, 24, 43, 64), quality time (5, 34, 37, 44, 47, 48, 57-60), and receiving gifts.

- Quality 38 – You've read Linda's "wait gain" chapter; I also devote an entire chapter to this, also called, "Wait Gain." This is more important than you might realize.

- Quality 8 – the "IT" factor. As I said above, "it" isn't something that you can easily explain (I try below) – "it" is something that you know. I am so incredibly thankful that God had me wait until His perfect timing to bring the one He kept for me into my life. As I look at all 67 things on this list, they all combine to form that "IT" factor.

You will have disagreements and you will endure fights. Linda and I have found that when we are discussing serious topics, making big decisions, or are ready to talk through a fight, the best thing we can do is to say a prayer asking for God to guide our conversation and our decision, and then hold hands while we talk. On November 3, 2018, two became one. Actually, three became one. We need to act like it.

After over five years of being together, and almost five years of marriage, and after everything Linda and I have been through together in that time, I actually can now tell you exactly what that "IT" factor is: it is the special someone that you know beyond a shadow of a doubt, beyond a 25%, 50%, or even 97% probability, will honor those marriage vows they made to you before God, your family, and your friends. And you know this is 100% certain because they have demonstrated it time and time again. They have made a decision, and showed you with words and actions, that their promises to you on your wedding day, these promises…

…To have and to hold from this day forward

…For better, for worse

…For richer, for poorer

…In sickness and in health

…To love and to cherish

…Forsaking all others

are indeed the things they will continue to do "until death do us part." That is the "IT" factor. And "IT" is definitely worth fighting for. "IT" is not an impossible dream.

Jesus also demonstrates that "IT" factor to us. He is always there, right by our side, for better or worse, for richer or poorer, in sickness and in health. He loves you. He cherishes you. He wants to have that lifelong relationship with you. While this list certainly helped me to find "the one," I am so incredibly thankful and blessed that "the One" found me!

CHAPTER 10

WAIT GAIN: A MAN'S PERSPECTIVE

Time is certainly an interesting thing, isn't it? As we've mentioned, it is hard to believe nine years have passed since I started writing the original book, and eight years since the original *God Knew* was published. And quite often when we think of time, we associate that with waiting. Linda told you about waiting in her story, but from a woman's perspective. Here is this man's perspective:

Most of us don't like waiting. Life is busy and we need to get things done. We want what we want when we want it. As a young child, when Christmas was approaching, we wanted to open our gifts *now*. But, our parents said, "You have to wait." Every day we'd ask, "How much longer?" The answer? "Be patient. Wait." We didn't understand why, but our parents knew the time just wasn't right for us to receive our gifts.

Or perhaps we wanted to eat all the cookies as they came right out of the oven. But, our parents said, "You have to wait." We were disappointed, but our mouths continued to water as we thought about eating tons of cookies. We'd ask, "How much longer?" Our parents knew the hot cookies would burn our tongues, and that too many cookies would give us a tummy ache. The time just wasn't right. And they also knew what wasn't good for us.

Our heavenly Father works in the same way. We see something we really want, and we pray to God to answer our prayers and give it to us...now! Sometimes, instead of waiting on God, and on His perfect timing, we just take what we want, not realizing it isn't good for us, and it's not what we really *need*. God has eternal reasons for saying, "Yes," "No," or "Wait (a/k/a not yet)" on our prayers. In fact, there are some things the Bible explicitly tells us we should wait for, because it is part of God's design for our lives, and His plans are always for our good.

I must warn you…I'm about to get into a controversial societal topic here. You may have a different opinion and you may even get upset with what I'm about to say. But, if this chapter gives some encouragement and strength to a young person, or even an older person, to follow God's Word and keep the faith, it is worth it. My comments are mainly directed to men since I have a guy's perspective on this, but women may find what I have to say helpful as well.

Okay, here is that controversial societal topic…waiting. I'm talking specifically about sex here. Perhaps not ironically, since God's commands and society's opinions frequently differ, waiting is not controversial in God's eyes. Sex is our Heavenly Father's gift for us…in marriage.

From an earthly perspective, God certainly took His sweet time bringing Linda and me together!! Many nights we soaked our pillows with tears from loneliness, wondering what was wrong with us. A failed relationship here, an unfulfilled passing fancy there, and we started to question God, "How much longer?" There was a temptation to abandon our morals, values, high standards, and God's Word and just take any relationship without waiting on God's timing...and His best.

Before we met, Linda and I both had opportunities to have sex outside of God's holy estate of marriage. Neither of us did. And I'm happy to say that Linda and I both made love for the first time, and the first time with each other, on our wedding night. Thank God we resisted that temptation (with others, and with each other)!! I should remind you that I was 50 and Linda was 48. That is a *loooong* time to wait!

So, why am I telling you this? We live in a society that, against God's Word, has normalized, promoted, and perverted sexuality and sexual relations. Here is one example: the Bible is very clear in Genesis 1:27 (NLT), *"So God created man in his own image, in the image of God he created him; male and female he created them."* There are only two genders, male and female, despite what society wants to deceive you into believing. The Bible is also very clear that sex is God's wedding gift to a married couple, with a married couple being one man and one woman. The Bible is timeless – it applies as much today as it did when it was written. I am not being judgmental, intolerant, or any other word someone may want to use. I am simply reminding you what God's Word says, and I believe God's Word is true. See the chapter later in this book on "I Can't Change the Terms" to learn more about this.

Did I handle all my relationships perfectly? No. After all, I am a guy. Hormones raged; temptations pursued. In some relationships, sometimes kissing got a little passionate, and sometimes hands wandered over parts of clothing and places they shouldn't have. And at times, willpower almost caved. Almost. Even Linda and I were tempted, once we were engaged to "go all the way," attempting to justify it in our minds that we were going to be married anyway, so why wait? That's how easily the world deceives us, and thankfully we recognized the deception.

I cannot stress this next point enough: the best way to not sin is to not put yourself in a position to sin. Let me repeat that: the best way to not sin is to not put yourself in a position to sin. Thankfully, God kept His promise that when we are tempted, He will provide a way out, an escape. And He did provide one every single time. 1 Corinthians 10:13 (ESV) says, *"No temptation has overtaken you that is not common to man. God is faithful, and he will not let you be tempted beyond your ability, but with the temptation, he will also provide the way of escape, that you may be able to endure it."*

I remember way back in high school listening to male classmates in the locker room talking about their latest sexual conquest. I remember a classmate in college talking about all the women he had conned into bed, and he was proud of it. I remember hearing conversations from coworkers, or guys at the golf course, talking about their exploits. I stayed out of those conversations for fear I would be asked about my "conquests," and when I told the truth that I didn't have any, I would be the subject of locker-room jokes and ridicule. Back in those days, in that fight (stand up and vocalize my values) or flight (hope they don't ask me) decision, I chose flight. Plus, when you are in high school, and even college, Satan will try desperately to convince you that girls only want guys with experience. As you will learn, in quite a few cases, that is a complete lie.

Television shows and movies promote promiscuity. They want you to abandon the waiting God may be calling you to endure, in exchange for instant gratification. The world says:

- "Look, everybody's doing it!"
- "You aren't hurting anyone."
- "There aren't any consequences – just pleasure."
- "You must be the last virgin on earth! What's wrong with you? What are you waiting for?"

Friend, the world lies.

It's that last lie that often got me. It's one thing to be lonely; it's quite another thing to be lonely, still a virgin, and living with the thought you might die that way. Pastor Shoup puts it in perspective this way: "sex is a gift from God. It is something beautiful that He wants us to enjoy in a marital relationship where He has joined a man and a woman together. If, however, God's will for your life is to remain single and not marry, your virginity is something you can give back to Him as a gift." There is no denying that is a very beautiful and pious thought, but it provides little comfort when facing the next how many years alone and without that level of intimacy, and you look at the empty space next to you in bed and realize that singleness might be a life-long sentence.

Guys, now I'm talking specifically to you. Remember these three things: 1) don't believe the lie that you are the last virgin on earth – you aren't; 2) don't believe the lie that everybody is doing it – they aren't, and 3) you gain so much in your relationship with the right woman by waiting. When the world tempts you with, "What are you waiting for?" you can respond, "I am following God's will for my life and I'm waiting for God's best; for the woman He created just for me. I don't care how long it takes." I'll copy the words from Linda's chapter: "that's easy for me to say…now."

For our Christmas letter in 2018, I chose Galatians 4:4-5 (ESV) as the Biblical theme, *"⁴But when the fullness of time had come, God sent forth his Son, born of woman, born under the law, to redeem those who were under the law, ⁵so that we might receive adoption as sons."* I did this for a reason - on November 26, 2017, the fullness of time came for Linda and me, and God said, "Your wait is over!" God used modern technology to bring us together. Our relationship formula started out as: 1 repeating TV commercial for eHarmony during Hallmark Christmas movies + 1 heartfelt sermon titled, "God's Got a Plan" by Pastor Jerry Brooks at Discover Church (listened to online) = 2 incredible souls meeting (the start of our own Hallmark movie!).

Linda and I had several phone conversations immediately after the initial email online. I knew from those talks that she was a very good person and that we shared many of the same beliefs, values, and morals. We met in person at a Panera Bread in Oak Creek a few weeks later on a Saturday afternoon. Linda was telling me about the men she had met online that only wanted three things: 1) a texting-only relationship; 2) money; or 3) sex. Again, this was our first in-person meeting. I was able to look her in the eye and respond, 'Well, the fact that I'm here shows you I don't just want a 'texting only' relationship. I have enough money of my own so I'm not looking for any help or handouts. And, at age 49, I'm still a virgin so I won't be asking you for sex." I wish I could describe for you the look on her face, but how do you describe a look that combines skepticism, relief, and *wow* all at once? She then verbally confirmed what I had suspected and hoped for when she said, "I am a virgin, too." She told me that she had made a pledge to God many years ago that she would remain a virgin until her wedding night.

Now, let me try to bring a few things together here:

1) If you are young (middle school, high school, college) – wait. Don't believe locker room stories, don't succumb to peer pressure, and don't listen to society's lies.

2) If you are older, still a virgin, and never married (like Linda and I were) – wait. Guys (again, I'm talking to you here), I've been there. Based on the women I was finding online, in Northeast Wisconsin, and through the professional matchmaking service, I had resigned myself to the belief that if God had somebody for me to marry, she would likely be divorced, with children. You get to a certain age, and you think you know what "fate" awaits you. How many single, never

married, virgin women are there after a certain age? Then, you can get into your head (like I did) – well, if that woman is divorced, it means she is not a virgin and she likely already had a lot of sex with her husband. And maybe she has had sex since the divorce, or before she was married. She's probably been with a rock star. Here I am – no experience whatsoever. How am I ever going to satisfy her sexually? She will be so disappointed with me. Maybe I should lie about being a virgin so they will go out with me (because who wants to date a 40-year-old virgin, right?). And once you get to that point, it's only 1.5 steps to the conclusion: "Well, if that's my fate, I better just find some woman to have meaningless sex with so I can get some experience. It will make me more desirable, and I won't feel so inadequate." How do I know this? I'll give you one guess who was very tempted to make this mistake! Even Linda said she was tempted to just go to a bar, pick up some random guy, and just get it over with. The temptations are all too real. So are the lies.

Look, I don't know who God has in mind for you. It might be God's plan for you to be single for the rest of your life. That's where my head was at between 2014 and 2017. I had resigned myself to just being a good Christian friend to those people that God put in my life. I've heard it said, and I've said it myself: if you want to make God laugh, tell Him your plans. God's plan might also be that you will end up marrying a divorced woman who has a lot more sexual experience than you have. You know what? If you are ultimately with the person God wants you to be with, it's all going to be okay. I'm sure you will have a lot of fun figuring things out. And if that is the woman God has for you, she will recognize, appreciate, and love that you had the courage to stand up for what God's Word says. It demonstrates your faith, your loyalty to Him, and your character. Your heart is what she is really after, not what's in your pants. And, who knows, you might also be blessed by God in giving you the gift of a virgin woman on your wedding night.

3) If you are a single woman, Jesus is not your boyfriend. If you are a man, Jesus is not your significant other. Jesus is your Savior. He is your friend. He is your strength, and He is your comfort. But He is not your girlfriend/boyfriend. Press into God's Word and follow God's plan for your life. Get the proper perspective on your relationship with the Father, Son, and Holy Spirit. If you are confused about this, please talk to a pastor that knows sound doctrine (be careful – there are some pastors out there who are more society-focused than Bible-focused).

4) Relationships are difficult. Relationships take work. I don't care what age you are when you get into a relationship, both of you are bringing some sort of "baggage" into that relationship. It's true that the more life you've lived, the more baggage you likely have. Linda and I, while never married before and not having any kids, still brought a lot of baggage to our marriage. But the one piece of baggage missing is the prior sex life. I feel safe in bed with Linda. I know she has given me the most precious wedding gift she could have given me; a gift I know she has given to no other man – her virginity. And she knows I gave her that same gift in return. I know I'm not being compared to anybody else, and she knows she is not being compared to anybody else. There is safety in that, and unless you've experienced it for yourself, it is difficult to put that into words.

There is one more thing that ties into #4 – fidelity. Faithfulness. I know that if Linda made that commitment to God to remain a virgin until her wedding night, and that she followed through on that commitment, I am confident that she will also remain faithful to me and her marriage vows. She vowed to "forsake all others, until death do us part." Because she took her sexuality so seriously, I know she will take it seriously and forsake all others for the rest of our lives. Again, she has the same comfort and assurance from me. There is a comfort in knowing that, especially in a world marked by disregard for marriage vows and the sanctity of the marriage bed.

5) Don't watch pornography or look at dirty magazines. It's all over the place but that doesn't mean you have to look at it. As I've stated twice earlier, the best way to not sin is to not put yourself in a position to sin. That junk is not reality. It really isn't. It poisons you and it will poison your current and future relationships. If you are addicted to porn right now, seek help in stopping.

6) This last one should be fairly obvious, but I'm going to say it anyway – as you know, words, once spoken, cannot be taken back. And your virginity, once given away, cannot be taken back. It is a physical, and psychological, impossibility. That is why it is such a gift from God – take care of it, and don't open it until your wedding night!

If you're still reading this incredibly long chapter, thank you. Obviously, the words are having an impact on you and are touching your heart. I thank God for that.

Now, there is a strong likelihood that some of you have not done things this way. Your virginity is just a distant memory. You didn't do things God's way. You let temptations and passions get the better of you. You wish you could have a do-over, but you know you can't (point #6 above). Or you were married and now are divorced. I have some good news for you. God's forgiveness covers your sins. It covers all of mine, too. As LCMS Pastor Bryan Wolfmueller says, "Jesus is a better Savior than you are a sinner." As I said, I didn't do things perfectly, but I know God forgives me. And if you are in a relationship that isn't how God designed relationships to be, you can repent and change things starting today. What? Yes, you could tell your girlfriend, or the woman you are living with, that you want to start doing your relationship God's way – no more sex until marriage. Yes, this sounds harsh and judgmental, I know, but if she doesn't want to do that, and wants to keep on having a relationship that is not pleasing in God's sight, and your heart feels convicted to do things God's way, she is probably not the right girl for you. And if she isn't the right woman for you, it's better to end it now than later. This same solution applies to women, too. Focus your efforts on finding a forever kind of love.

It occurred to me while writing that some of you reading this may not have given your virginity and innocence away by choice. It was taken from you. If that is you, I am so sorry. If that is you, and it's getting in the way of you having a normal relationship, please seek help from a Bible-preaching Christian pastor or Christian counselor. You are not damaged. You are not undeserving of love. You are God's precious child. He loves you and He wants what is best for you. In His perfect timing, He will make it happen. He loves you with a forever kind of love.

Speaking of forever love, that's exactly what found us at Christmas: God's forever love for us. The people of the Old Testament waited and waited for the promised Savior to arrive. They asked, "How long, O LORD, how long?" In God's perfect timing (in the fullness of time), the waiting game was over, and God gave us His best...our Savior was born. Jesus. Immanuel. God with us. And on Good Friday, even death could not part us because the Savior arose on Easter Sunday, victorious over sin and death! We wait expectantly for Jesus to come back. We ask, "How much longer?" In God's perfect timing, Jesus will return again and take us to Heaven, to live with Him there. Our waiting game will be over, and we will receive God's best, as, through faith in Jesus, we have received adoption as sons and daughters!

It is because of Jesus that we have the forgiveness for our sins. All of them. Even the sexual sins we have committed in the past. Look to Jesus, follow God's Word and His plan for your relationship, and you will obtain a prize that will definitely be worth the wait. You will delight in His faithfulness fulfilled.

CHAPTER 11
THE WAIT IS OVER

"³Trust in the Lord and do good; dwell in the land and enjoy safe pasture. ⁴Take delight in the Lord, and he will give you the desires of your heart." Psalm 37:3-4 (NIV)

Once upon a time, there was a prince named James…Jim for short. He lived in a kingdom far up north in Green Bay Packers country and he was successful in all he did. Despite his success, he lacked one thing…a princess to share his life with. But God knew. You see, there was a princess that lived in the southern kingdom in Milwaukee Brewers country, and she was in the same boat. She had patiently prayed for her prince and God answered her prayer, and He answered the prince's prayer, too.

I have heard it said, "Once in a while, right in the middle of an ordinary life, Love gives us a fairytale" and, cheesy as it sounds, I finally believe it. So, what did Jim's and my fairytale look like? Well, I thought you'd never ask.

It all began a couple of weeks before Thanksgiving 2017. I had received an email on eHarmony, although I was no longer a subscriber. Because I was curious, I checked out the person's profile and quickly realized that he and I weren't a match. Interestingly though, I was practically blinded by a bright, blinking, neon message telling me that "if I would just subscribe again for 3 more months, I could get it at an outrageously low cost!" and something (or Someone) told me to subscribe again (for just one more time). I decided that I would give eHarmony one more chance, and then after that three months' time, if I didn't meet someone, I was going to give up and maybe start a cat collection. But God knew better, and He had arranged this encounter. And this is how the fairy tale began.

It was the Sunday morning after Thanksgiving 2017, and I was at home tuning into church online that day. I had been very busy the week before with rehearsals for a Christmas musical my church was doing starting the following weekend, not to mention preparing for Thanksgiving with my family. Also, I attended *Hamilton* in Chicago the day before with a big group of friends from church. So, you can see…I was busy! But not too busy to tune into church, where Pastor Brooks was doing a sermon series called "God's Got a Plan."

It was the last message of the series, and he shared a very personal, soul-stirring message about how our prayers sometimes seemingly go unanswered for a long period of time, or sometimes don't materialize the way we hoped for. When that happens, it's easy to feel bewildered or frustrated. But he also reminded us that God is a good God, and no matter what, we shouldn't give up. Why? Because God is faithful, has good plans for our lives, and we can dare to believe that He will take care of us...in a way we would never be able to conceive.

I was so there in that place that while bawling my eyes out, I prayed and surrendered that part of my life over to him fully. I wanted to stop fretting about it, and I wanted Him to take over. If my *"but God You promised"* prayer was to be realized, and if He had someone that He had in mind for me (the one He kept for me), to please send him to me. The method of delivery didn't matter - it could be via FedEx, UPS, USPS, homing pigeon…I didn't care; just send him. And I finally fully turned my desire for someone to love and to have someone love me over to God. I literally opened my hands and lifted that desire and handed it to Him. I sat in His presence until the tears dried from my cheeks and I just trusted Him.

After the service was over, I began working on decorating my Christmas tree while watching Christmas movies on the Hallmark Channel, only to find out later that Jim was sitting at his computer also likely watching/listening to the same Christmas movie I was watching at the very same time. While watching, he kept hearing the white-haired older gentleman who was the spokesman for eHarmony reminding everyone that it was free communication weekend, and you could message your matches for free during that time, so he decided to follow the advice and take a look.

And there I was, the first profile to come up in his feed...blurry face, red scarf, and all. Because, as Jim has shared in his chapters of this book, he has been lovingly described by some of his close friends as "tighter than bark on a tree" when it comes to spending his hard-earned money (he's really not—he just doesn't like spending it on himself). He wasn't a subscriber to the site and, couldn't see my photo fully, but he remembered seeing that same picture on another site a year earlier, recognizing my curly blonde hair and the red scarf I was wearing. But when he saw my profile on the other site, he noticed that I lived over two hours away from where he lived and just felt that the distance was too great to consider contacting me just then. However, this day, he read my profile and decided to take a chance and message me anyway. Couldn't hurt, right? The worst I could do was say no, or just ignore the message altogether. And so, he took a chance and sent the message.

As you can imagine, my heart jumped in my throat and I kind of freaked out for a minute when I saw that I had a message on eHarmony, being that it was only 2 hours after I had called out to God and surrendered this part of my life fully to Him! I even looked around and up at the ceiling of my living room like *is this from You, God?* Truly believing that it was from Him, I sat down at my computer and responded to Jim's message. Because we were both busy at the time, and both had plans that evening, we set up a time to speak over the phone a few days later. Like on the phone! No texting, no emailing... but actually talking! How refreshing!

Tuesday afternoon came, and my phone rang. During that phone conversation, which lasted over two and a half hours, we realized very quickly just how much we had in common. Like tons in common. You see, Jim had never married either, and had taken care of both his father and his mother until they passed. He loves Jesus, loves the Hallmark Channel (right?!?!), loves the Packers, has an amazing sense of humor, and was also looking for his soulmate; the one he would spend the rest of his life with. Just like I was.

We talked to each other several times in the week or so after our first call. I shared with him that I had a part in the Christmas musical at my church and asked him if he might want to come see it and we could have our first meeting then. So, the plans were made that he would come down the following Friday. He would drive down and stay with his friends, Paul and Kristi, who you met in the first *God Knew* book. Paul was his best friend from their elementary years, and they had remained close ever since. Paul would tell the story later that he knew this was something big because Jim never came down to the "big city" to visit. Paul and Kristi would always visit with him when they came back to Shawano, where Paul's parents still live. The fact that Jim was willingly making the trip and asking to stay with them (again, tight, bark, tree) was a momentous occasion.

So, Jim made the trek down to Oak Creek and settled himself into his seat at church. He will tell you he was nervous and almost got up and left, wondering what in the world he was doing there. He knew there was such a distance between where he lived and I lived, and questioned if he even wanted to possibly start something that would end up turning into a long-distance relationship. But God had other plans. He told Jim soundly to keep his booty in the pew and he watched the girl with the curly blonde hair and red scarf playing the part of the "Fishmonger" in a Christian version of what happened to Tiny Tim after he grew up. Her character was brash and loud, and she grumbled a lot. She wore a pair of cut-off gloves and had soot on her face with a messy wig covering that curly blonde hair. In case you're wondering just how messy that girl looked, well here's a photo (I am the one on the right), mugging with my castmate and good friend Mandy.

Truly the best way to meet your possible new beau, right?? But God has a sense of humor, and this certainly was a great example of that!

But that dirty-faced, loudmouthed fishmonger didn't scare him off, and Jim did come out to meet me after the performance was over. We made plans to meet again for coffee the next morning at Panera Bread and had another great discussion about our lives and how we got to be who we were at that time. It was during that conversation that Jim asked me again about past boyfriends and previous dating experiences. I had told him that there wasn't all that much to tell, and that my online dating experience wasn't a positive one. I mentioned how I had felt like most of the men I was in communication with seemingly only wanted one thing and it was the one thing I was not going to give them. I didn't want to be treated like an object and Jim confirmed that he was not that type of guy. He then confessed to me that he had dealt with the same things and that he also had made a commitment to God when he was young to keep his virginity for his wife and he had done so. And I confessed I had done the same.

I'm guessing that surprises many of you. How in the world could two people, whose ages added up to almost 100 years old still be virgins in this day and age? The answer really is simple: with God's help. We each had a gift that we wanted to be able to give only to the one we would marry. It wasn't easy and we weren't perfect in this area, but up until this point, we had kept that vow and we were thankful we had.

We realized at that moment that this was something special and that we definitely wanted to continue learning more about and getting to know each other. In fact, we talked so long that I was almost late for my 2:00 p.m. performance of that same musical I told you about earlier! We quickly said our goodbyes and continued talking on the phone just about daily. And it was during one of those conversations that Jim decided to come back down for New Year's Eve, and we would have our first official date. And so began the crazy life of a long-distance relationship.

Because we lived so far away from each other, we would trade off weekends; one weekend he would come down to visit me and the next I would head up north to visit him. Some weekends we would meet halfway and just spend the day going to a movie and sharing dinner, taking a drive, or just find a nice spot to walk around and talk. And each weeknight, since we couldn't be together physically, we found ourselves talking on the phone usually for three hours straight, and texting each other often during the day, as well. We had waited for so long for this and we had much time to make up!

We both knew not long after our first date that we had found each other's Mr./Mrs. Betterhalf. We just knew. Then, on the first weekend I came up to visit Jim, three weeks into the new year of 2018, Jim took my face in his hands and told me he loved me. It was so sweet, and, feeling the same way myself, I said it back to him, too. And for the first time, those words truly felt real, and knowing they were reciprocated, made them all that more special.

We began introducing each other to our family and friends. It truly was a whirlwind! As those we loved watched us falling in love, they were so supportive and really wanted to get to know the person that was the answer to each of our prayers: theirs, mine, and Jim's. Our friends were quick to share their approval and were so happy and excited to see where this road would lead. They would join us on the ride and would partner with us in prayer for God to lead us into our new life together.

As Song of Solomon 3: 1-4a (Berean Standard Bible) states, *"¹On my bed at night I sought the one I love; I sought him but did not find him. ²I will arise now and go about the city, through the streets and squares. I will seek the one I love. So, I sought him but did not find him. ³I encountered the watchmen on their rounds of the city: 'Have you seen the one I love?' ⁴I had just passed them when I found the one I love. I held him and would not let go…"*

Jim and I had both seemingly gone through the streets and squares through online dating and other avenues, seeking the one whom we would love. We prayed countless prayers and cried limitless tears. We climbed mountains and walked through dark valleys. We had waited, and we had finally found it. And we would never let go.

CHAPTER 12
THE ONE WHERE THEY GOT ENGAGED

"And I will betroth you to me forever. I will betroth you to me in righteousness and in justice, in steadfast love and in mercy." Hosea 2:19 (ESV)

Are you still with me? I know we've covered some heavy subjects up until now, and I am so excited to continue to share how God wrote the next part of our story. I had a pastor/friend once who used to tease me and my friend Penny because we would be telling a story and we'd say, "This is really good…but this is even better." It seemed like every story was super good or funny. But then we always could find something else that seemed even better. So, if the last chapter was "really good" (and I hope you think so), then "this is even better." Now, we've covered how Jim and I met and how our relationship started, but what happened next?

Well, on the weekend of Valentine's Day in 2018, Jim surprised me with tickets to Disney on Ice in Green Bay. And before any of you start thinking *"That's for little kids,"* you obviously haven't met the girl who really, really loved Disney. I named my dog that, for Pete's sake. Anyhow, it was very sweet and romantic, and we had an amazing time.

After the show, we decided, being that we were in the Frozen Tundra of Green Bay, we needed an inside outing to burn some time before dinner, so we headed to the mall. As we were walking through, we started to pass by Rogers & Hollands jewelry store and instead of walking by, Jim took my hand and led me into the store. He thought it would be fun to just "look." Because he's a guy, he didn't understand the significance of what it means to take a girl into a jewelry store to just "look" at engagement rings. So, we sat down at the counter, and we looked and commented on several of the settings, and it was then when I saw it…The Verragio. I tried it on, and I knew it was "the" ring. It looked like Cinderella's carriage from the side, made with white gold with rose gold and diamond accents along the inside, and it was beautiful. I kept flashing it around and brushing my bangs to the side while looking in the mirror (in the meantime, my "tighter than bark on a tree" boyfriend was looking at the price tag!). Let's be honest ladies, I am not the only one who has ever done this. Needless to say, it was not easy to pry that beautiful ring off of my finger at the time, but we had dinner reservations, and the store was closing, so I had no choice but to give it up to the salesperson, and we headed out to our Valentine's Day dinner.

It was kind of early to think about engagement rings anyway, right?

As the days and weeks went by, we continued to get to know each other, and our feelings of love grew. We found about a million more things that we have in common. We realized that we both have dreams of serving God and others and were certain that God had brought us together. It just became more and more apparent to us that we wanted to share our lives together.

Come March, Jim took me to look at several other rings at other stores and then he said the words, "The Verragio is still in play." And that was all folks. At the risk of sounding shallow and greedy, I would ask for some grace here. I was 47 years old, almost 48, and this was the first time I had ever gone into a jewelry store for the purpose of finding a ring that would symbolize and be the outward sign that I had found my love and was binding myself to him for the remainder of my life. And my heart told me that The Verragio was the one I wanted to grace my finger for all my days. So, we found ourselves back at Rogers & Hollands once again. We looked at men's rings at that time, too, and found the one that suited Jim. No purchases were made but plans started forming in our minds all the same.

We began talking in earnest about marriage and thinking about possible dates. We quickly came to the conclusion that it was now April and, if we didn't want to continue with the long-distance situation (which was getting harder and harder on us because we wanted to be together all the time), we needed to decide on a date soon. And because we live in said Frozen Tundra and our people are half of a state apart, waiting until early in 2019 wasn't an option due to fickle weather conditions. We also knew that we *really* did not want to wait until after the snow finally ended in the Spring because that would be a full year away.

Because we wanted to have a big wedding where our friends and family could join us and share in our happiness, we decided to go for it and chose November 3, 2018, as our wedding date. The main ceremony would take place at my home church in Oak Creek, and then, because there were many who might not be able to make the 2.5-hour trip from up north, we would have an affirmation of vows ceremony at Jim's church (St. Paul Lutheran) in Bonduel two weeks later. That way, we would each be married at the churches we were currently attending, and, for Jim, in front of the same altar his parents were married. One decision down – we had a date (and another), so what was next?

Saying "yes to the dress" of course! And, before I hear any of you saying, "Umm, excuse, me, but are you even engaged yet?" the answer to that question is, no…not yet. But as I mentioned before, we knew. We had a date, and said the date was a mere 6 months away and everyone knows that you need like two years to plan a big wedding, and friends…we were planning two not-so-small weddings! This girl did not have time to be waiting on a proposal and a ring. We had to make hay when the sun was shining, as they say. (Who is "they" by the way? Always wondered that.)

Anyway, I found a dress designer that I loved, and on April 8 a store in Chicago was having a pop-up dress sale. Since Chicago is only about an hour away from where I lived, I loaded up two of my bridesmaids (yes, I already had those lined up, too—remember, I was like Monica on *Friends* and had been planning my wedding in my head for years) and we drove down to try on dresses. I mean, I wasn't buying one yet…I was just seeing what was out there, right? I really *was* just looking.

I should also mention that just before I met Jim, I had started a very regimented and strict eating program. I had lost about 55 pounds at this point, with plans to lose quite a bit more, so I was trying on dresses knowing that I was going to be losing quite a bit more weight before the big day. Way to add pressure and stress to an already tight schedule and life, I know. But God was my ever-present help!

And then I saw it…*The* Dress. It was perfect! And everyone in that store, and I do mean everyone, said it was perfect. Strangers were stopping in their tracks and telling me that the one I was currently wearing whilst standing on the pedestal was THE DRESS. But it couldn't be because I wasn't buying a dress that day. But then I did. Because it was perfect. And, I could get $200 off only if I ordered it that very day (scoundrels). When I told them when our dates were, they were very clear that to have that dress made for me (and 2 sizes smaller I might add because of planned weight loss), I had to order that dress that day to ensure there was time enough for alterations before the wedding date we chose. So really, I had no other choice but to buy it that day, right?

Well, Jim now loves to tell the story that basically *I* asked *him* to marry me because at this point, we had dates picked out, I had a ring picked out, and now I had the dress. I just needed to be asked, and since he was taking his ever-loving time, I would have to do the asking, too. Well, he loves to tell it that way, but that's not how it really happened.

Jim had said all along that he wanted to be traditional and ask my dad for my hand. I loved that because, first of all, I knew my dad would love to be asked, and secondly, because it was really very romantic to think about. It's not something people do much anymore, I'll bet, especially at our age, but it just felt right.

One thing I mentioned earlier was that Jim and I, whether we were together in Shawano or Oak Creek, would always meet up with friends and family so they could get to know us since we would both be incorporated into each other's friend groups once we were married. But doing so didn't allow for a lot of alone dates for us. As such, in the middle of May, Jim reminded me that we hadn't been on a proper date in a while, one where we dressed up and went somewhere nice, just the two of us. Therefore, the "proper date" on May 18 was added to our calendars.

So, Jim headed down to pick me up after work for our date. Since I usually drove to work and parked in a parking structure downtown, we agreed that I would take the bus in that day so we wouldn't have two cars downtown after dinner. That morning, I loaded up my work stuff, along with my dress, heels, curling iron, and make-up to change and get ready after work, and hopped on the bus. Fridays were casual, so I made sure I brought things along with me to get fancy for our dinner that night. As I was taking the elevator down with my friend Cathy, I mentioned our dinner and she asked if we were getting engaged that night. I told her no because Jim hadn't asked my dad yet, and he said he was going to do that before he proposed.

I exited the building and there he was, waiting for me across the street from my office. I jumped into his car, and we headed to the restaurant, which was still a surprise at this point. Having lived in that area and working downtown, I had an idea after a bit of where we might be headed, but he was cool about it and wasn't offering any confirmation. It turns out, we were a little early, so he pulled the car over and reached back into the back seat, and then handed me a red rose, saying that a proper date required a red rose (how cute is that?). And then, coincidentally, one of his favorite songs from one of his favorite artists, George Strait, called *"I Cross My Heart"* happened to come on the radio. Jim proceeded to serenade me with words that were so perfect and special. Perhaps I was totally clueless, sleep-deprived, or whatever, but I truly did not expect what was soon to come.

About 15 minutes later, we arrived at the restaurant, and he said that since we were still early, maybe we could walk around the back of the restaurant and look at Lake Michigan while we waited for our reservation. Of course, me, being the practical girl I was, promptly told him sure, but I wasn't walking down all those stairs to the lake (we were on a high bluff) in my dress and heels. Instead, we compromised by going down just 12 of those steps to a little open area and he put his arm around me to look out toward the lake.

He started talking about how beautiful it was, but then his phone started buzzing incessantly, so he thought it might be an emergency and maybe he should just take the call. So, as any curious girl would do, I started looking around and looked back at the restaurant above us to see what was going on up there. To my surprise, I saw a photographer with a lens up to his face, seemingly taking photos of the lake. I whipped around and told Jim that there was a photographer up there and that we were likely in his shot of the lake he was taking. Because I'm just that slow.

Anyhow, after rolling his eyes, he turns me back around toward the lake and then asked me if I wanted to dance with him. I said yes and so he hit play on his phone and the song *"Marry Me"* by Train starts playing. And then the lightbulb FINALLY went on and I look back up and see the photographer, and then see Jim on one knee in front of me, where he has a ring…The Verragio…in a box and he tells me he loves me very much and asked me five life-changing words: "Linda, will you marry me?" I looked around, realizing at that very moment that what I had been dreaming of for so long was finally happening and it felt like a Hallmark moment…I turned back toward him, put my hands up to my face because I truly couldn't believe it, and (after what Jim would say was 15 minutes later), I said YES! I should mention here that Jim completely doubts that story to this day based on the picture below, but I really was surprised and just looked away a moment to see if anyone in the restaurant was watching what was happening.

Photo credit to Craig John Photography.

After he got up off his knee (not 15 minutes later) I thought for a moment and said, "what is my dad going to say?" He just laughed and said he had already asked him, had gotten his blessing, and would tell me that part of the story later.

Then the manager of the restaurant walked out with two glasses of celebratory champagne, and we toasted our engagement. And, yes, it turned out the photographer, my friend Craig, was there to take our engagement pictures. After the photos were taken, we headed inside the restaurant for an amazing dinner at a table by the window overlooking Lake Michigan and the spot Jim proposed. At the table was a bouquet of daisies (my favorite flower) and six more roses to add to the one Jim had already given me earlier in the car for a total of seven roses. Seven because that is God's number and the number of completion, and because we both felt that our marriage would only be successful if it is centered around God.

After dinner, we stopped at Starbucks, grabbed a coffee drink, and pulled up Facebook to do a live video. We shared our engagement story and our friends and family joined in and were so excited for us. They had been waiting and praying for us for so long, too! After closing Starbucks (what rascals we were), we went back to my home where I had to hide my hand as much as I could while Jim brought in his luggage. I knew my dad had an idea that we had gotten engaged, though, because he kept looking to see if my hand had something shiny on it. It took a few minutes, but after Jim finally got settled, we shared our news with Dad, and he was very happy for us.

Funny story, though…I mentioned before that Jim had planned to ask my dad for my hand, and so one night about a month or so earlier, he slipped out of the guest room at our house to do just that. Now, you have to know that my dad was not one for surprises. He needed time to get used to ideas. When Jim asked him if he had his blessing to ask for my hand in marriage, my dad's initial response was "I think so." To verify, Jim asked the question again and he answered again, "I think so." As you can imagine, Jim did not take that as a ringing endorsement, so, before he made all the plans for the restaurant, etc., he felt he needed to revisit that discussion with my dad again. A couple of weeks later, he got to my house before I did after work and he asked my dad again… and that time, Dad answered with a resounding "Yes!"

Remember when I said that my pastor was also like a second dad to me? Well, Jim decided to go the extra mile (which many of you who know him will not be surprised) and asked Pastor Jerry, too. Thankfully, and not surprisingly, Pastor Jerry gave his blessing as well. I like to think that meant a lot to him, too.

Engagement photo – May 18, 2018.
Photo credit to Craig John Photography.

And before I move on, I must tell you the infamous story about the first ring...the "Not-Verragio." So, because Jim figured that since we had all the major wedding plans figured out already and that nothing was really going to be a surprise, maybe he could still surprise me with the ring. Even though he knew that I really loved The Verragio, that maybe it would be better if he chose *another* ring instead...so that at least *something* would be a surprise. So, he went to a special event that Rogers & Hollands was having and found a different setting, chose the diamond, purchased it, and picked it up about 10 days before he planned to propose. But then the doubts set in. So, he casually brought up the subject by asking me, "I know you love The Verragio, but what if I picked out another ring for you? Do you think you could love it, too? Because I want you to love it and be proud of it and show it off to all your friends." And I sat there speechless, because how do you really answer a question like that? I mean, yes, I did love The Verragio, but how shallow would it make me sound to say that it was The Verragio or nothing? So, I told him I wasn't answering that question. He asked me again the next day and told him (and it was true) that I would love any ring that he chose because it came from him and out of his love for me. But then he kept pressing me...for another couple of days, saying, "But honey, I want you to love it and if you didn't like it after you saw it, I could take it back and get you the one that you would love and be proud of." Finally, after three days, and in exasperation, I answered him and asked why he would risk it then, getting me one that he knew was not the one I had made clear was my favorite. Because once I had a ring on my finger from him and he proposed, there was no way in heck that ring was coming off my hand. So, he took back the surprise ring and, although they had to jump through some major hoops, they were able to get him The Verragio in time for the engagement.

I shared that story to be funny, well, because it is. And because it shows just how much of a loving man Jim really is. I pray that after all you have learned about me up until now, you will see that I love to give my ring a proper name, but that is out of humor. Don't get me wrong, I do love my engagement and wedding rings, and I am very proud to show them off to any and all who want to see them, but I truly would have loved any ring that Jim chose for me. Because it's truly not about the ring; it's about the love that the ring represents. But the story is too good not to share, so share it I did.

Now that we got that story told, it was time to plan.

CHAPTER 13
WE SAID "I DO" (TWICE)

"Therefore a man shall leave his father and mother and hold fast to his wife, and the two shall become one flesh." Ephesians 5:3 (ESV)

Remember when I said I was like Monica on *"Friends,"* and I had my whole wedding planned in my mind since I was a teenager? Well, it's one thing to have it in your mind…it's another thing altogether to execute. But we had some amazing friends and family who rallied around us, and Jim and I hit the ground running. The countdown began – 5 months and roughly 15 days to go for our first wedding and then just about 6 months until our affirmation of vows that we would have at Jim's church. He always wanted to get married in front of the same altar that his parents had married in front of 54 years prior.

Of course…that second date just happened to be on the opening day of gun deer hunting season in Wisconsin. Them's fightin' words up here in the Northwoods, and you can bet we heard that from many of our male (and female) friends (it is up north after all), but the dates worked with the church, the caterer, and the reception hall, so it was set all the same.

We chose our wedding party, five on each side. My best friend, Tammi, would be my matron of honor, and Jim's close friend (and Pastor) Tim Shoup would be his best man. All the other members of the wedding party were amazingly important to us (both friends and family members), had made an impact on our lives, and had cheered us on during all our years of waiting. One of my bridesmaids, Faith, was supposed to be my flower girl had I gotten married 20 years prior. But since she was now married and a mommy to two children at the time, well, asking her to be my flower girl would have been just weird…not that the thought hadn't crossed my mind just the same. Good thing I had a practical-thinking fiancée who put his foot down, and so a bridesmaid she became.

Bridesmaid dresses were picked out, groomsmen suits ordered, and fittings scheduled, flowers and a cake were chosen, and then we worked with another friend, Katie, on our invitations. She was an amazing crafter, and together we designed a very elegant invitation. And, in August, we recruited a group of friends to help, and we put them all together and hand-addressed every one. Since Jim and I were not young'uns anymore, we had a lot of friends that we wanted to share in our celebration. My list was 220 and Jim's was 300. That was a whole lot of glue dots, envelope stuffing, and sticking, and calligraphy-ing (not exactly a word, but you get it). At long last, the invitations were compiled and ready to be mailed out.

Jim's very good friends, Keith & Kelly Baumann, who own a restaurant and banquet hall up here in Shawano, agreed to cater both of our receptions in Oak Creek and in Shawano—truly a blessing, especially traveling the 167 miles to Oak Creek to do so. We are ever grateful to them for doing so!

Thankfully, Discover Church has a very large hall (well, a gym really) that could accommodate up to 500 people and was extremely affordable, so we booked it for our first reception. We worked with the church to use their decorations to turn a very stark, cold space into a gorgeous, intimate setting, which included up lighting and Christmas trees. I had to fight for those, and fight I did. Who wouldn't want to have white twinkle-lighted Christmas trees to make the space look perfect?

It was a crazy five months of planning, and finally, the responses began to pour in. I had an intricate system for who would be coming to which ceremony/reception and how many, different colored highlighters for each date, and a cute box with dividers to keep everything straight.

Sounds all blissful and wonderful, right? Like a total dream come true with no pitfalls? Well, that wasn't the case. At the end of June, just a couple of days after my 48th birthday, I heard a crash in the night and then Dad yelling out in pain. I flew out of my bed and found him on the floor of his room; he had fallen and broken his hip. He would need to have a pin put in and would have to be in rehab for a couple of months for it to heal and to get his strength back.

Now you can imagine, I felt horribly for him and the pain that he was enduring, but it was also very stressful for me too. I was working 25 minutes away and had to ask a neighbor to check on Disney throughout the day, and there was also the worry on my mind about what was going to happen to him when I moved away three months later. Would he heal enough to stay in the family home, or would he need to move into an assisted living center? Not to mention the question as to whether my dad would be able to walk me down the aisle. I know that probably sounds selfish, and it likely was a little bit. I had waited so long to have my dad give me away and I wasn't sure that would be able to happen now. It was an emotional time altogether.

In the event that Dad wouldn't be able to make it home, we started looking at assisted living centers and found one that seemed perfect if it was determined that was the route that would need to be taken. In the end, that endeavor would prove to be very fruitful, but that's a story for another chapter.

Thankfully, since Dad was highly motivated by the thought of walking me down the aisle, he used that as his goal in rehab, and worked hard to get back on his feet. That motivation paid off and he was able to come home in late September. I was still worried if he would be alright at home by himself after I moved, but God gave me peace about it. My other family members were nearby, and they would help him out as needed.

Also, at the same time, because God has a perfect sense of timing (and humor), He knew just where my breaking point was. I was planning two weddings, my dad had a traumatic health event, my fiancée and I were still only seeing each other on weekends while making the final arrangements for two weddings from separate places, I was health coaching and continuing to work full time, so God, at the perfect time, gave me a major Godwink.

The Tuesday after Labor Day, I was told I was being let go from my job due to budget cuts. Since my employer knew I was getting married and moving anyway, they killed two birds with one stone and chose to cut my position. For most people, this would be a crushing blow and another major stress issue, but for me, it *was* a Godsend. Why? Because now I had time to finish planning my wedding, make room for me in my fiancée's home, get my dad settled at home, and begin interviewing for a new job in my soon-to-be new hometown. I could not have done any of those things as easily had I remained employed. Thankfully, because I had been with my company for 18 years, I received a very nice severance that would carry me well into the spring of the following year. The time to start my new life had come and it was another example of joy coming from suffering.

Speaking of joy, remember when I was wondering if the day would ever come when it might be my turn to have the bridal shower and wedding? Well, God, being faithful and loving as He always is, gave me not one, not two, but four showers and a bachelorette party! He heard my prayer for just one shower, and because He always wants to show off and show His goodness, He quadrupled that request. He's just such a loving God like that.

Then after five months of planning and waiting, the big day was about to be here. We had our rehearsal and dinner at the church the night before, then fell into a heap, exhausted and excited for the next day – the day that Jim would change my name, and our life together as man and wife would begin.

The wedding was at 2 p.m. and I met with my hair stylist and makeup artist at the church at 9:30 a.m. My bridesmaids would get there around 11 a.m. and then everything would start happening very quickly. We had photos planned with our respective wedding parties before the ceremony, so we had to be ready by 12:30 p.m. to get those photos done. Jim and I decided we wanted to be traditional and not have a first look, but we did decide to have a first prayer. After the photos were taken with the bridesmaids and groomsmen, we met in a hallway at the church and held hands around the corner to share a prayer before the ceremony began to ask God to bless the day to come and the vows that we would take just a few minutes later.

Photo credit to Christy Janeczko Photography.

After our prayer, Jim went off with Pastor Brooks and his groomsmen, and my bridesmaids and I followed a few minutes later toward the sanctuary. Everyone was lined up and ready, and I met my dad in the lobby all set for the doors to open and for him to walk me down the aisle to meet my groom-to-be. Dad looked so debonair in his suit and tie. Nestled within my floral bouquet was one of my mom's necklaces, so I had her there with me, too. It wasn't the same as having her with me that day, and I missed her so much, but I knew she was watching and cheering from heaven. And my heart was happy.

Photo credit to Christy Janeczko Photography.

The ceremony was beautiful. Together, we picked out songs that were important to us, and we had some of our favorite people sing them. We had chosen traditional scriptures and Pastor Brooks spoke some very personal and touching words that only a second father and long-time pastor could share. My dad was super cute taking photos from the front row on his flip phone, and then Jim and I spoke our vows, built our unity cross, and then the ceremony ended with, Pastor Brooks sharing five more life-changing words to Jim, "you may kiss your bride." And kiss me he did! We then exited the platform to the tune of the Hallelujah Chorus. Years of waiting were over; Jim was my husband, and I was his wife. And it was good.

Photo credit to Christy Janeczko Photography.

After the ceremony, we had pictures at the church and at a local park, and then came back to the dinner and reception. The food was delicious (thanks Keith & Kelly), the cake was beautiful and tasted even better (thank you Aggie!), the speeches were fun and touching, and we got to greet so many friends, family, and loved ones. It was exhausting and magical and we would not trade a second of it. God was so good, and He was there in our midst the whole time – the Third Strand, just as we had asked Him to be.

After all the hugs were given, the cake was eaten, and the dress removed (thank goodness—it was beautiful but not made for sitting), the reception was over, and we made our way to our hotel. And for the first time, as man and wife, we gave each other the gift that we vowed to save only for our spouse. We had waited to share the ultimate act of intimacy as a married couple, and it was blessed.

The next day, we boarded a plane to Florida and headed out on a Disney cruise for our honeymoon. The weather was beautiful, the room with the balcony was perfect, the food was amazing, and it was such a great way to rest after a very busy year. For a few blissful days, we felt like there was not a care in the world. After spending a few additional days at Disney World, we made our way back to reality. We packed up our cars with our suitcases, Jim's suit and my dress, some of our wedding gifts, my dog, and we headed out on our new adventure…our new life together in what became our home.

Our affirmation of vows ceremony was held several days later and so my family headed up to Shawano and Jim and I got to stand again together before God, friends, and family and re-affirm the vows we had taken just two weeks prior, but this time in front of the altar at St. Paul Lutheran Church. Because Jim's best man, Pastor Shoup, was now officiating the ceremony, and a couple of my bridesmaids couldn't make it, we had to do some re-shuffling and adding an impromptu bridesmaid, but it was a beautiful ceremony, as well.

After it was over, we headed to the reception where I would have my first dance with my husband, and then I had my daddy/daughter dance to the song *"Fathers and Daughters"* by Michael Bolton. Dad could only stay on his feet for a few minutes before we had to get him a chair, but it's a memory that I will cherish forever in my mind and heart (and on video, thanks to my brother Jim). "Fathers and daughters never say goodbye"…words that bring tears today at this writing, but they were perfect then.

And that's the story of the end of one era of our lives and the start of a new life to come. Jim had gained a second earthly Dad, and many brothers and sisters, nieces and nephews, and new friends, and I had gained a few aunts and uncles and cousins and new friends, too. God had united two people into one flesh and had united two families and blended them into one. The one difficult thing is that Disney didn't do well at our new home and "Grandpa" was missing his girl, so she went home with my dad when they went home after the Affirmation ceremony. This mama's heart broke that day (and for several years after really), but sometimes Mama's need to do the hard things when it's the best thing for our babies.

Speaking of moms, Jim and I have an image in our minds of our moms getting together and pulling Jesus to the edge of heaven and pointing down to each of their kids and asking, "You see those two…can you make that happen?" There are those who don't necessarily think that is scriptural or doctrinally sound, but for Jim and me, well, we believe that is exactly what could have happened. God had heard the prayers of our moms, asking for Him to make a way so that their kids wouldn't walk through this life alone. And He made a way for those roads that were so far apart to meet. Because God knew.

Photo credit to Christy Janeczko Photography.

P.S. These were my wedding shoes, bedazzled by our friend Diana. Although they represent shoes that could be worn to walk along the road of life, these beauties were not meant for just any old road.

CHAPTER 14
WEDDING DAY LETTERS

Having been to many marriage ceremonies, but having never been involved in planning a wedding, there are certain "behind the scenes" things that take place that are surprising, but also very special.

Our videographer, Danielle, asked both Linda and me to write a letter that we would share with each other on the evening of our wedding day. These are not public letters, but letters to each other, written from the heart, to try to put our story, and our love, into words. She then had us do an audio recording of those letters and blended them as a voice-over to various parts of our wedding highlight video she produced. That video is available on our website.

Linda and I felt it would be appropriate to share those letters with you. Here is Linda's letter to me:

"My Dearest Jim,

How do I even begin to put into words how thankful I am to God for bringing you into my life? He heard my fervent prayer last November, asking him to bring to me the one that he had kept for me, and on that very day, within mere hours, He prompted you to contact me. He had already written our amazing story and was just waiting until our hearts were ready to receive His blessing. I will be forever grateful for His faithfulness.

Jim, I have said this many times, but you are my earthly rock. You are strong where I am weak; your smile brightens my day, and your strong arms help me feel safe. Your kind and generous heart is awe-inspiring to me. You are my best friend; the first person I think about in the morning and the last person I think about at night. I love our nightly marathon phone conversations, most times talking for three hours or more just so we feel connected living so far apart and only seeing each other on weekends. I love that we have the ability to talk about anything, even if it's hard because we know doing so will make us stronger.

I love your tenacity, wanting to get to the true heart of matters even if it frustrates me at times. I love that you know that I am like an onion with a lot of layers, but even so, you love me and are not afraid to peel off the layers one by one.

I love how committed you are to your family and how you would do anything for them. You didn't grow up with brothers and sisters or nieces and nephews but now you have them in spades. And while your earthly dad has gone to heaven, you now have a dad again. One thing that drew me to you more than anything else was the sacrifice you made by taking care of your parents for so many years. I know first-hand what that sacrifice means, and while that was a sacrifice, it was also done with an open heart and open hands. You honored your mom and dad, and God is blessing you now because of that.

On our first date for coffee, you mentioned to me that you had written a book called "God Knew." I couldn't wait to read it because I knew doing so would give me great insight into who you were inside. As I read each page, I could just see what a sensitive, good-hearted, loving, compassionate, and responsible man you were.

As we both found out by dipping our toes into the world of online dating, finding someone real who possesses those qualities is a very rare thing. God knew just the person I would need to complete me, and he saved you for me and me for you.

And now we stand here today before God and our friends and family promising to love, honor and cherish each other forever and always. Jim, I want you to know I choose you and I'll choose you over and over and over. It has been said once in a while in an ordinary life, God gives us a fairytale. And I cannot wait for ours to begin. I love you, my Darling.

Your loving wife, Linda"

Here is my letter to Linda:

"My Darling Linda,

God knew.

Our long wait and our search are finally over. The Bible says, "I have found the one whom my soul loves." (Song of Solomon, 3:4).

It's sometimes hard to believe our wedding day is finally here...a day both of us have hoped for, dreamed of, and prayed for as long as we can remember. Along the way, we have both experienced heartache, pain, and loneliness. We have both been tempted to give up. We both wondered if there was somebody out there for us to love, and who would love us in return.

But God knew.

Sunday, November 26, 2017, is a day that changed both of our lives forever. I love our love story – a story of two souls that God finally brought together in His perfect timing. We didn't know if He was going to answer our prayers for a Christian spouse...but God knew.

Linda, the past eleven months have been some of the best of my life. We have had some really fun times. And, we've had our share of challenging times, too. But we've always turned to each other to talk it out, and to work through it, and to come out stronger on the other side. We both gave grace and received grace. We also kept God as the center of our relationship. Thank you for loving me!

My darling, you truly are my Miss Amazing. You are one of the most loving, caring, loyal, compassionate, family-oriented, Jesus-loving, Jesus-following, fun, Christian women I have ever met! And you are as beautiful on the outside as you are on the inside. We share a love and a bond that is rare. I am extremely blessed, and I thank God every day for the gift of you. You make me want to be a better person. I doubted if a woman existed that would meet my incredibly high standards. But God knew – He made you especially for me.

By the time you read this letter, we will be married. We will have spoken our marriage vows in front of God and our family and friends...vows where we promised –

- *To have and to hold*
- *For better, for worse*
- *For richer, for poorer*
- *In sickness and in health*
- *To love and to cherish*
- *Forsaking all others*
- *Until death do us part*

I'd like to add a few vows of my own. I vow to –

- *Be the spiritual leader of our home*
- *Pray for you, and with you, every day*
- *Keep God as the third and most important strand in our marriage, binding us together*
- *Communicate with you, whether good news or bad*
- *Like you*
- *Keep our lives fun and interesting*
- *Be your protector and defender*
- *Be your best friend and confidante*
- *Be your most valiant supporter and cheerleader*
- *Show grace every day*
- *Love you more each day*
- *Always tell you and show you I love you*

I won't be perfect in this, but with God's daily help and grace, I vow to be the best husband for you I can possibly be.

Grow old with me, Linda...I believe the best is yet to be! God has some amazing plans for our future.

What are those plans?

God only knows!

I love you, Mine! Forever and always!

Your husband, Jim"

Have I been the perfect husband and always gotten everything just right? I think we all know the answer to that. None of us do everything perfectly. But with God's help, I have certainly tried to fulfill each and every one of these vows. I love Linda more today than I did on the day I wrote this letter.

One of the lessons I've learned in the almost five years we've been married is to make sure God remains an integral part of our marriage...not Someone on the periphery, but the One in the center. Good times? Celebrate with God and thank Him. Bad times? Press in even closer to God. All times? Don't forget He is *always* there.

On our wedding day, Linda and I received many special gifts, and we appreciate every one of them. But, more importantly, we appreciate the special people that celebrated our special days with us. One of those gifts was so incredibly special and heartfelt that I want to share it with you. It ties in so very well with what I've been sharing with you.

In *God Knew, Revelations of God's Grace in Unexpected Ways*, you read about my best friend growing up, Paul Frisque. You know how special Paul was in my history, how vital he was when my mom was dying, and the great friend he continues to be in my present. Paul was a groomsman at our wedding. He and his wife, Kristi, created a beautiful, handmade gift for us. They made us this framed picture, which hangs in our bedroom, as a reminder of who we are, Whose we are, and the gentle reminder of Who makes a marriage successful. As you know, I'm LCMS Lutheran and Linda is Assemblies of God, and their gift honors both of those with a pencil-drawn outside picture of Discover Church on the left, the altar of St. Paul Bonduel on the right, and a wedding picture in the middle. Incredibly fitting is the cross at the top, the ever-present reminder of the One who is ever present with us, and Who loved us so much that He died on the cross to save us. We will cherish this gift, and God's gift to us, forever:

CHAPTER 15
"HOME SWEET HOME"

When you've been single for almost fifty years, you tend to get into certain habits that are difficult to break. I believe the politically correct term is "set in your ways," while other people might use stubborn and inflexible. All would be accurate. While Linda and I were single all our lives, neither one of us had much experience living alone (my exception would be the few years between my mom dying and getting married to Linda). When you get married (and even before that), you quickly learn that you won't always get your way (and that's okay) and that a relationship works best when you can compromise and work together to determine what is best for your future together. The following story illustrates that very well.

As you've read, Shawano (Northeast Wisconsin) and Oak Creek (Southeast Wisconsin) are approximately 167 miles apart (around 2 ½ hours by car). Linda was born and raised in Oak Creek, and I was born and raised in Shawano. While both of our jobs are equally important, my success as a business banker is much more dependent upon long-standing relationships in the community. Linda's job at an appraisal company is quite different. Because of my established relationship network, we decided it would be better for Linda to move "up north" than for me to move south. Ironically, Linda's desire had always been to move much farther south in the U.S. to someplace warm and sunny with no snow. Who knew that she would fall in love with a guy that lives even farther north than she does? God knew!

For over 18 years, Linda would commute to work in downtown Milwaukee from her home in Oak Creek. On really good days it took her about a half-hour each way, depending on traffic. My commute in Shawano was much different – about 3 minutes each way. Linda would say I was spoiled, and, in fact, I was. For over 30 years, my commute from home to work has been 3 minutes or less. Plus, traffic in Shawano is never a consideration!

Initially, when Linda informed her employer in Milwaukee that she was getting married and intended to move to Shawano, her boss told her they would make arrangements for her to continue with the company and work remotely (keep in mind this was 2018, two years before working remotely was a big thing). We were excited – Linda could keep her pay, her vacation, and her tenure, and she wouldn't have to learn a new job on top of all the other pending changes. However, once corporate HR in New York heard about it, they said they couldn't allow that. Well, that just added a lot more to a plate already overflowing with stress. Linda did not know how she was going to be able to finalize wedding plans, coordinate her move to Shawano, keep working in Milwaukee, start interviewing for a new job up here, and keep her sanity in the process.

But God knew.

As Linda told you, even though the company knew Linda was going to be giving her notice and quitting, they needed to make budget cuts, so her position was eliminated. However, since she hadn't given her official notice, they offered her a six-month severance package, with an end date of September 20, 2018. This allowed Linda to leave her job, still get paid for the next six months, and focus her time and effort on interviewing, the final wedding plans, and making the move north. That really was a blessing from God.

After being with her company for that long, Linda was making a decent salary – higher than what companies in Shawano were likely to pay. So, we decided that she should focus her efforts on finding a job in Green Bay or DePere, which are about 30-40 minutes east of Shawano. They are bigger cities with more opportunities, and a higher wage base. I reached out to my network of business associates, and they were more than happy to connect Linda to potential employers. She began interviewing in the fall of 2018, a few weeks before we got married. Most of her interviews were in the Green Bay and DePere areas.

Now, I will admit that there was a strong temptation for me to just keep my mouth shut and be selfish. Linda was already accustomed to a 30–40-minute daily commute and who would want to give up a

3-minute commute? But that is not how God wired me. It wasn't a fair arrangement. I knew I would worry about her, especially in the winter, risking her life on snow/ice-covered highways while I dealt with one right turn and one left turn on city streets. Plus, she had agreed to move up to Shawano for me, leaving her dad, dog, family, and friends to basically start over. She was leaving the only home and community she'd ever known. I felt I had to give up something in return, even if it meant giving up the same things, like moving from the home where I had lived for over 20 years and moving from the only community I've ever known. Also, part of the agreement was that we would visit her dad and family in Oak Creek at least one weekend a month.

There is another component here I should mention: while Linda liked my home in Shawano, she viewed it as just that...*my* home. Even if she moved into this house after we were married, it wouldn't be *our* home. If she was going to move to start our life together, it would be *our* life and *our* home.

Ultimately, we agreed to look for our new home in the Hobart area, which is between Shawano and Green Bay. I would have about a 20-minute commute back to Shawano and Linda's would be about the same to Green Bay/DePere. My then-manager's wife, Michele, is a long-time successful, ethical realtor in Green Bay (and a great friend) so we gave Michele the task of finding us a house to live in – a house we could turn into *our* home.

It didn't take long for Michele to find a "For Sale by Owner" property in a great subdivision in Hobart. We toured the property and immediately fell in love with it. We found out the young couple selling it were Christian, and we got to meet them and tell them our story when we did a subsequent home tour. Michele found some other houses for us to tour in the same neighborhood, but none of them measured up to the first house.

The listing price was higher than I had hoped for. I almost had my home in Shawano completely paid for, so going into big mortgage debt again, and potentially becoming house poor, was not something that I was looking forward to. But fair is fair, and a deal is a deal, and it was the right thing to do.

You probably know, like me, that God has a sense of humor. I've experienced it many times (and you've read about some of those times). So, I had a hunch this house situation could turn out to be another one of those times. I thought, "Wouldn't it be something if we put an offer in on this Hobart house, and Linda ends up finding a good job in Shawano after all? We would both then be commuting 20-30 minutes from Hobart to Shawano, instead of just being in Shawano and having a short commute."

We met with Michele and decided to put in an offer on that house, contingent upon the usual things – financing, appraisal, inspection, etc. Then, we asked Michele to add another contingency – a contingency she had never added in over 16 years of being a realtor. We told her to add a contingency that we would only purchase the home if Linda found a job in Green Bay, DePere, or Hobart by December 31, 2018. If she didn't, we could cancel the contract. Michele didn't know if the sellers would go for something like that.

But God knew.

On October 27, 2018, literally one week before our wedding, the sellers accepted the offer, mainly because they liked our *God Knew* story of how we met, and they were Christians who also believe God works all things together for our good. It was a very happy time as things were all falling into place, and everything was going according to our plans.

Fast forward through the month of November 2018, which included our official wedding, a Disney cruise and Disney World for our honeymoon, and the affirmation of vows ceremony at St. Paul. You read about those in other chapters. Meanwhile, interviews and follow-up interviews continued. Then, one by one, doors started closing on Linda's job opportunities. The newlyweds were starting to get nervous again.

I came home from work on a Monday night in early December to find Linda sitting in the living room, crying. That is a sight no husband ever wants to see. I took her in my arms and asked what was wrong. She said she had just heard back from her last job opportunity that "they were going in a different direction." She had no job prospects anymore. She was sad and nervous and said, "What's going to happen to the house we put an offer on? We are supposed to close at the end of the month, and I've got nothing! What are we going to do? I don't want to lose that house." I held her and reassured her that everything was going to be okay. I put on a brave face and said comforting words, even though I had no idea how things would work out.

I can't tell you how many times in my life I've had "no idea."

But God knew.

In the subsequent chapter, Linda will share the "God knew" story of God working to get her a fantastic job opportunity (so I won't steal any of that thunder here), but it wasn't in Green Bay, DePere, or Hobart. You guessed it – it was in Shawano! Thank God (literally) for that contingency in the offer to purchase.

Our next call was to Michele to tell her our good news, and to have her inform the sellers we were backing out of the offer to purchase. They completely understood and were happy Linda found a great job. We found out later they ended up selling the home the following February for more money than what we offered. God is good that way.

You might think this story can't get any more amazing, but it does. Now, I'll be like Paul Harvey and tell you "The rest of the story."

With Linda and I both now working in Shawano, we still faced the dilemma of "our house." We did look at some other homes in the Shawano area, but nothing caught our attention. We then decided maybe God wanted us to stay in our Shawano home and do a remodel instead. So, we looked at various options, but nothing seemed quite right. There was a lot of give and take in our discussions of what we wanted (remember: tight, bark, tree). Then Michele mentioned she often works with a contractor in Shawano, who I had never heard of, that does great work at reasonable prices and gave us his contact information. He came over and we told him what we were thinking. A few days later, he came back to us with his price, which surprisingly was within this cheapskate's target budget. So, from May through October 2019, we lived in a construction/remodel zone, with Linda trying to work remotely with all the mess and commotion. Everything turned out extremely well (better than we imagined) and it is like we are living in a new home. The before and after pictures show we truly transformed *my* home into *our* home. And our new mortgage is less than half of what it would have been if we had purchased the home in Hobart.

Now, for the icing on this cake. Remember when I told you in an earlier chapter about Denmark State Bank in Shawano going from an LPO to a limited-service branch to a full-service branch? Well, in December 2018, the same week that Linda accepted her new remote job, the president of Denmark signed an offer to purchase that full-service bank branch, which is…wait for it… only two blocks away from our home! We can literally see the branch from our living room window.

My commute to work is now about 30 seconds. Linda basically has to commute from our bedroom to the family room. We are living in *our* home. And we are not "mortgage poor." In all those things, we didn't know where all the pieces would end up. But God knew. And His plans for Linda's job and our house far exceeded our plans. If we have a choice between our plan coming together, and His plan coming together, we will take His plan every single time.

CHAPTER 16
THE TRUTH ABOUT FAIRYTALES

"⁹Two are better than one, because they have a good return for their labor: ¹⁰If either of them falls down, one can help the other up. But pity anyone who falls and has no one to help them up. ¹¹Also, if two lie down together, they will keep warm. But how can one keep warm alone? ¹²Though one may be overpowered, two can defend themselves. A cord of three strands is not quickly broken." Ecclesiastes 4:9-12 (NIV)

So, it is true? Is finally marrying the man/woman of your dreams the end-all, be-all? Does it make life perfect? I [Linda] think you all know the answer to that.

The first few months of our marriage, while mostly blissful, also came with some struggles. It was harder than I anticipated to leave friends, family, my church, and the only home I had ever known to move to a brand-new place to start a new life with my husband. Also, Jim and I had lived independently for a long time and figuring out how to blend our personalities and ways of doing things wasn't always easy. We found out the hard way not to make assumptions about certain things. For example, I would get annoyed when Jim would leave his socks in the living room, and Jim would get annoyed with me when I would redo his placement of dishes in the dishwasher to fit more in. I would get frustrated when Jim would put dishes away in the wrong places because there was a spot open, and Jim would get frustrated when I would leave water in a bowl in the sink to soak them and not just spray them out or scrub them clean right away.

Seemingly, little things, but when you are dealing with the stress of moving and sharing spaces that we'd never had to share before, those little things seemed very big, and frustrations built, and "discussions" ensued. But when we finally communicated the reasons why we did all those things, it made so much sense and we realized we got frustrated with each other for no good reason. We learned quickly not to "major in minor things."

I know Jim shared our story in the previous chapter about the accepted offer we had on the home near Green Bay and my job search, so I won't go into major detail about the home miracle in this chapter. However, when it came to my job search, while there were jobs available, there was nothing with a salary anywhere near what I had been making where I had lived. This was very difficult for me emotionally because I felt like I had worked so hard for so many years, and to take such a cut in pay felt so demoralizing. And so, I did what I always do – I prayed. Well, honestly, I cried and then I prayed. God was faithful yet again, which led to another "God knew" moment.

You see, after all the options I had available had dried up, I felt defeated. It had never taken me more than one interview to get a job before. To make things worse, I had been sick with a major sinus infection and a terrible cough for several weeks at that point, and with my defenses down, the defeated feeling was magnified.

Jim came home from work that night to find me in tears, and we prayed right there that God would bring the right position for me with a salary that I was more accustomed to. And because God is so good, just two days later, I received an email from a recruiter from a competitor of the company that I had worked at for the previous 18 years. They had been given my name by a former co-worker of mine. I was excited to hear from them, but the position was located in a city close to where I just moved from. I responded to her that I was interested but I couldn't make the commute. However, if it was ever available as a remote work situation, I would be interested. The recruiter called me back 30 minutes later and said that due to my previous experience, a remote working situation was a possibility. We arranged for me to interview the following week.

As I entered the office, I was greeted by one of my former co-workers! It turned out that I had previously worked with four of the five people who were in that office that day, including the person I was interviewing with! Oh, and did I mention that the job had become available just two weeks before (another placeholder story)? The interview went well, and I was offered the position the next day! I was overjoyed that I would be able to work at home, and they matched my salary and vacation time to boot!

God knew that the transition I was going through with leaving my family, my home, my church, my previous job, my friends, and my dog was harder for me than I realized it would be. So, He brought me into a situation where I could have a modicum of the familiar. I would start after the first of the new year, which allowed me time to continue to get settled in my new home and to celebrate the Christmas season with my family without the worries of missing work.

Meanwhile, Jim told you how his bank purchased the new building we could see from our living room window, which they would move into within a couple of months. So, had we purchased the home we had the accepted offer on near Green Bay, we would have had to move, I would be working out of our new home and Jim would have had to commute 35 minutes each way to the bank that was 2 blocks from our old home.

What an amazing God! He knew just the perfect situation that both Jim and I needed, and He was faithful in making it happen. Honestly, you just can't make these things up! And being able to walk through all these life events together, with God as the Third Strand, made such an amazing difference. We clung to each other and supported each other through every one of these situations.

After that, life started to settle into a more normal routine. I made the 15-step commute into my office and Jim made the two-block commute to his new bank branch. We had a weekly date night, and we spent our weekends making breakfast together, seeing movies, attending concerts and the theater, double dating with friends and, once a month, going back to Oak Creek to visit my family and friends. And, because life comes full-circle, I even drove a float for Jim's bank down Main Street in Shawano for our annual hometown Christmas parade, while Jim walked behind throwing out candy to the kids along the sidewalks…talk about Hallmark moments!

We continue to attend church at St. Paul Lutheran Church so that Jim can continue to worship how he is accustomed to, and we also began faithfully attending Hope Community Church, which has the type of worship I had always experienced. It is a practice that we will continue to follow for the rest of our lives together.

Because we hadn't had enough change in our short marriage, as Jim mentioned, in May of 2019 we began a six-month, full-home remodel project. The project ultimately turned out amazing, but it sure brought some serious upheaval while it was happening. There was not a room on our entire main floor that wasn't touched. At one point, we had no cabinets, no stove, and no kitchen sink, so we were eating grab-and-go items for breakfast, peanut butter and jelly sandwiches for lunch, and we ate out every evening. This went on for six months. I was working at home throughout the whole endeavor, which was great for answering contractor questions, but not great for staying on task at work. It was a crazy time but, in the end, we had a home that was "ours." God had blessed us beyond measure, and we continue with our plans to utilize our home for ministry, and for making people feel loved and welcomed.

The fairy tale continued, but little did we know what was to come in just a few short months…

CHAPTER 17
AND THEN THE WORLD
CHANGED FOREVER

"Even when I walk, through the darkest valley, I will not be afraid, for you are close beside me, Your rod and your staff, protect and comfort me." Psalms 23:4 (NLT)

2020 – a year that will live in infamy; the year that changed life as we know it forever. Not just for us, but for the entire world. And everything just turned gray for a while. That's how it felt to me [Linda] anyway. Life as we all knew it just stopped and we were all frightened because this was not something any of us had ever encountered before. It was such an unknown. Jim and I often said to each other that we were so thankful we had each other during that time because it would have been very daunting trying to maneuver through those days alone. There was so much fear that was rampant during those days and if we hadn't had each other to cling to, it would have been so much scarier.

I am not going to complain at all about how difficult things were for us. We were beyond fortunate to live in a place that didn't have a huge outbreak of the C-word. It would not be until May or June of that year that we even had any major cases arise. We were careful when we had to go out, and we remained safe from sickness. Thanks be to God that no one in our family got sick in those first two years of the pandemic. We were all careful and we made it safely through. And though several of my family members lived within miles of the Kenosha riots, no one was harmed. We were blessed, and we do not take that blessing for granted.

We, like everyone else, started watching church online and only went out if we really had to. It was during that time I started digging even more deeply into reading God's Word and studying intercessory prayer. The things that began happening in our world were fearful to so many, including me, so I started looking for teachings and messages of encouragement to reassure myself God was truly in control of what was going on around us. And in all of that digging and studying, I found hope. I truly believe that no matter what the enemy tries to throw at us, he is a defeated foe. As Isaiah 54:17 (NIV) states, *"...no weapon forged against you will prevail, and you will refute every tongue that accuses you. This is the heritage of the servants of the LORD, and this is their vindication from me,' declares the LORD,"* just like the necklace I got as a little girl said. He promised in His Word not to ever leave us or forsake us, and I stand on that promise every day.

We stuck close to home like most people did, but finally, in May of 2020, we started visiting my dad again. He was an avid news watcher, so 2020 and 2021 were very scary for him. And since he lived alone, he just spent his days watching TV. Previously, when we would visit, we pretty much just stayed there with him and didn't see friends. We also decided to watch church online so that Dad could hear the sermons from Pastor Jerry and hopefully help him to see that when we have Christ in our hearts, we don't have to fear. Over the years, his heart had softened toward God, and after watching those online services, we would talk about the messages. There were a few times when I asked him if he knew for sure that Jesus was in his heart and that if he left this earth he would go to heaven. He would tell me that he did believe and that he just didn't demonstrate it like the rest of us did. And my heart was lightened because I became more confident that my dad would go to heaven after he died, and we could live together forever in eternity.

Just after we were married, Pastor Jerry asked if either of us had ever been to the Sight and Sound Theater in Branson. Neither of us had, and he told us then that we had to make plans to visit there someday. The Sight and Sound Theater is a Christian theater that performs Broadway-type shows based on the lives of the heroes of the faith in the Bible. The show at that time was *Jesus* (the Hero of all heroes) and we decided we wanted to try to plan a trip to visit Branson. Because we were still technically in the pandemic and we didn't want to deal with flying, in September of 2021, we decided to take a driving trip to Branson, Missouri. We did go to see *Jesus* at the Sight and Sound Theater (such a beautiful show and venue) and took in some of the popular shows and scenic tours, as well. We had no idea how beautiful it was there, and we fell in love with the locale, the people, the patriotism, and the Christian values that area of the country possesses.

And, because we could, and because we had such an amazing time in September, we planned another trip to visit there at Christmas of 2021. We even checked out some condos in the event that we might have the opportunity to purchase one and rent it out during the time we weren't there. It was a very fun trip, but was crazy busy with visitors hustling and bustling, but also, sadly, visitors who carried the C-word. Yep, after almost two years of dodging it, Jim and I we were bitten by the Omicron bug and had to cut our trip short. It was a fairly bad case for both of us, but, thankfully, neither of us had to go to the hospital. We just laid low for over a month and gradually the symptoms dissipated, and we began to feel better and were able to function again.

In the spring of 2022, my dad's health began to go noticeably downhill. When we visited, we could tell that he walked a lot slower than normal, and he would get tired and winded quickly just walking from room to room. He was still living in the family home at the time and was still taking care of Disney. But then in April of 2022, he received some very bad news which would pretty much drive the narrative for our family for the remainder of that year. My Dad had become very weak and had to be admitted to the VA hospital, where he was diagnosed with congestive heart failure with a calcified heart valve. The doctors told us that he had anywhere from one month to one year to live, although those same doctors told him it would likely be closer to six months.

As you can imagine, the news was crushing, so I decided to drive down to stay with him after he was released to the hospital while we determined the next steps that would need to be taken. Thankfully, I was able to work from my dad's house and I could also stay with him so that he wasn't alone.

Over the next three weeks, we arranged for Dad to be placed in hospice care and I contacted the same assisted living center that we had looked at before our wedding when Dad had broken his hip. Thankfully, they had availability and were currently running a special where Dad could rent a two-bedroom unit for the price of a one-bedroom unit. This was a Godsend because then Jim and I could use his second bedroom and stay with him when we visited.

Making the decision to move him to the assisted living center did not come without turmoil, though, because Dad did not want to leave his home that he had built over 50 years prior, and he really didn't want to give up his independence. But none of us kids could live with him to take care of him, so the contract was signed, and plans were made to move him in—all within three weeks of his diagnosis.

My three sisters, a sister-in-law, and I all pitched in to begin packing up his things and determining what items he would take along with him. Unfortunately, we just had to take control and make all the decisions because every time we would ask him anything, he would just say, "I don't know, I just don't want to do this. It's going too fast." It was heartbreaking to watch. Trying to work there during those three weeks was very difficult, too. There were so many CNAs and nurses and social workers coming and going and then other family members visiting throughout the day that it became a very stressful time. Jim was back in Shawano working most of the time, too, which made it even more difficult.

But finally, Dad's things were all packed and loaded onto the moving truck. Thankfully, we have a lot of boys in our family, and we were able to get him moved in and his things arranged and set up within several hours. The next day, I was able to go back home to my husband with Disney in tow. It was bittersweet because I was so happy to have my girl back with me, but she did not handle the transition well. For several months, she was terrified and withdrawn and spent most of her time hiding in a corner of our living room or next to (and practically under) my side of the bed in our bedroom. She missed her home, and she missed her grandpa.

Over the next several months, I made many trips back down to help clean out the house, bringing Disney with me so she could see Dad. Because Jim's home was very established, and because we had gotten so many shower/wedding gifts, I hadn't brought much up with me when I moved to Shawano. As I needed things, I would bring them back home after a visit, but I had the majority of 48 years' worth of my life still in that home. As you can imagine, those were painstaking days that garnered many laughs from old photos and yearbooks, and other items that brought fond memories, but also finding cards and trinkets from my mom that caused buckets of tears, too. Our family knew this day would come eventually. Dad was 88 years old. But the reality happened so quickly, and it took an emotional toll on me and my family members, but we kept at it. By the end of July, we had the home cleaned out and it was sold to a neighbor friend who would gut it and flip it. Now another family lives there and the house looks nothing like the home where we grew up.

As for Dad, he moved into the assisted living center, but his heart never left our home. He lost all desire to do any of the things that he used to do, and over the next several months, he became very depressed and barely ate or drank anything; just enough to take his medications and, because of that, his health declined very quickly. By late summer, we were told to begin making end-of-life arrangements for him. Thankfully, Jim and I and Disney were able to come visit every other weekend and it gave us time to look through photo albums and hear stories of his life and to be together before the time came to say, not goodbye, but "see you later." We had many talks with him during those months to ensure that he knew what it meant to confess Jesus as His Savior and that he would be reunited with my mom, brother, grandparents, and, most importantly, Jesus, when he moved from this world.

Sadly, that day happened sooner than we envisioned, and on November 2, 2022, Dad went to be with Jesus. I headed down to Milwaukee the following day—on our 4-year wedding anniversary. Jim joined me the following day and we finalized the funeral plans as a family. The funeral was scheduled for the following Tuesday, and I decided to give a tribute to my dad. Because I wasn't sure if I'd be able to make it through it, Jim agreed to stand by my side, and he gave a loving tribute, as well. Here is the tribute I shared:

"I really didn't think I would have the strength to come up here and share about who my dad was and what he meant to me and so many others in this room. I thought it would be too hard and too emotional and I would cry…which I likely will. But then I remembered how much he sacrificed for our family and the love he had for each and every one of us, and I couldn't not do this to honor him. So, I brought my husband, Jim, with me for moral support.

My dad was a very good man, but he was not perfect. There were difficult times that we as a family endured. But not one of us could say that he wasn't a good dad and that he didn't love us. He worked very hard to keep a roof over our heads and to put food on the table. He took on part-time jobs over his main full-time job just so he could provide for our needs. He made sure that we lived in a safe neighborhood and that we were home by the time the streetlights came on. Our home was often a gathering place for friends because they felt safe there, too.

As I looked through photo albums to put the photo boards together, it became abundantly clear to me that I was a "Daddy's girl." I was also a "Mama's girl," but I was truly a "Daddy's girl." There were countless photos of me sitting next to him in his brown recliner, most often asleep with my head on his chest…because he was a place of safety to me. I always knew I didn't have to worry, because Daddy was there, and he would protect me.

After we lost Mom, and we were both living in the family home, Dad and I would have our weekly dinners at Culver's and Perkins—because he always had coupons for both. He would tell me stories about taking on a paper route as a young man so he could have spending money, and how he and his friends, and then with my mom, would ride their Harleys up to Devil's Lake and climb the bluffs. Or of taking trips to Maine with his mom and his brother, Phil, to see their family home, and his time in the Airforce. He was a proud veteran and loved to wear his Korean War vet hat out and about.

When he was diagnosed with cancer and was sick, I prayed so hard for God to heal him, and He did. And when he broke his hip after I had gotten engaged, he worked very hard to get back on his feet and to heal. He would tell them that at physical therapy. "I have to get better, because my daughter needs her daddy to walk her down the aisle in a couple of months." He worked hard and did just that because it was important to him. And I did get to have my "Daddy/Daughter" dance with him at our Shawano reception. Part of it was from a chair with me standing beside him, but he tried, so that I could have and cherish those memories for the rest of my life.

When I would come down to visit each month, he would always remind me to give him a call when I got home because, "Daddy's still worry about their kids, no matter how old they get." If I forgot to call or it took longer than he expected, he would call me, just to make sure I made it home safely – all because he loved his kids.

There was a quiet strength to him. He was fiercely independent, even to his detriment sometimes. He was so proud of the fact that he could still get on a ladder at 80 years old to clean out his gutters....to our amazing chagrin and frustration. We would tell him, "that's what strong grandsons are for Dad!" But he never wanted to stop trying to do things on his own. He fought hard for that independence and in his last month's that's the one thing that bothered him the most; that he couldn't keep doing what he always used to do. He hated feeling inadequate.

I am so thankful, though, that he did give one thing up...his life to Jesus. I would ask him often after we watched the online services from Discover Church on Sunday mornings if he knew if he was ready to go to heaven when God decided it was time for him to come home, and he would tell me he was a believer and knew that Jesus was in his heart. He was quiet about it, and said he wasn't demonstrative about it like we are, but he believed. And for that I am so grateful. Because I know that he is now with Jesus, and he and Mom and Keith and our grandparents and other family members are interceding for their family here on earth. That we would know Jesus and trust in Him and give our lives over to Him, so that we can all share a very large block of mansions someday singing terrible versions of Happy Birthday and celebrating Christmas and anniversaries for all of eternity... together again as a family.

We [his family] are Dad's and Mom's legacy now. It's up to us to carry on the love and the values that he and Mom instilled in us into future generations. Let's take up that mantle together...because in Jesus, we are mighty and can do great things for God's kingdom until He comes."

There were many tears and some laughter, especially after Jim's tribute, which you will read in another chapter, but Dad's life needed to be honored. And we did just that.

The committal was the following day. We had arranged for him to receive military honors, which was so surreal and special to all our family. Dad had lived a long life; he was no longer suffering, and He was with Jesus.

After the funeral was over and his apartment cleaned out, Jim and I had a quiet Thanksgiving together, just the two of us. We had always celebrated together at the family home, but we didn't have that home anymore. And because I had Disney, it was just easier to stay home. We decorated for the holidays, even though they were quieter than usual, and tried to focus on the true Reason for the Season. We celebrated Christmas in Shawano with Jim's family, and then, heartbreakingly, I had to say goodbye to my Disney three days after Christmas.

That year, 2022, had been a very rough year. It started with sickness and ended in death. My heart was hurting, and I was so thankful that I had Jim with me to walk through those dark days together. However, as I had so many other times in my life when trials came, I leaned on God and trusted in Him, and He gave me the strength to make it through.

CHAPTER 18
"A TRIBUTE TO MY FATHER-IN-LAW"

As you know from *God Knew*, on August 7, 2012, God lovingly took my dad, Ralph, by the hand, and brought him Home. On February 25, 2014, He did the same thing with my mom, Lorraine. You read about my last days with my parents, the intense grief I felt after their passing, and how God walked beside me every step of my grief journey. I have found this saying to be incredibly true, "Time doesn't heal all wounds, but it does make the hurt bearable."

Can I tell you a little "not so secret" secret? I miss them every day, and sometimes a tear rolls down my cheek because they aren't here. Gerard Way said, "Tears are words the heart can't express." An unknown author said, "Tears are how our heart speaks when our lips simply cannot find the words to describe the pain we feel."

Can I also tell you a "secret" secret? After that initial intense pain…after that "gut-wrenching, my heart literally hurts from grief" stage…after that "I don't see how my life will go on" phase, there did come a weird sense of relief. It's almost selfish in a way; it's cathartic in another. I realized that I was never, ever going to have that exact, intense pain ever again. My parents cannot die again. Friends would experience the death of a parent and I would sympathize, even empathize, and think, "*I feel sorry for you, but I've been there, done that. I never have to live through the pain of losing my mom or my dad ever again.*" I had survived the worst thing imaginable, and I was now immune.

I'm pretty sure God looked down from heaven at me, His sometimes-delusional son, smiled, and said, "Oh, really?"

As the saying goes, "You don't just marry the person, you marry the whole family." That is so incredibly true.

When I married Linda, I was blessed with not only a wife, but also with brothers and sisters (that I'd never had before), and…wait for it…a dad (again). Richard Leighton wasn't a father-in-law – he was a dad to me. He treated me like I was his son, not somebody who had married into the family. It was neat to have conversations with him, and, yes, exchange infamous "dad jokes." I felt loved and respected by him. I hope he felt the same from me.

And then one day it happened – the realization that I had a dad again, maybe not biologically but certainly by heart, and unless Jesus came back first or decided to call me home first, I was going to have to live through that heart-wrenching, gut-punching, brain-numbing pain of death all over again. In other words, the price of love would need to be paid.

That anticipated pain became real on November 2, 2022, when God called Dad to glory. It wasn't an easy road to get there, and as Linda described, his last several months were marked with feelings of inadequacy and hopelessness as his body slowly wore out.

Hopelessness. Those who are in Christ are never without hope – hope in this world, and certain hope in the next. Dad readily admitted to us that he wasn't as demonstrative in his faith as we are, but that he believed in Jesus as his Savior. He would watch Discover Church online with us when we were visiting for a weekend, but he rarely talked about his faith. About a month before his death, he and I had a very open, faith-filled conversation early on a Sunday morning, and I could tell his faith was real, and that his faith was in Christ.

Prior to his funeral, my wife asked her family if anybody was willing to get up at the funeral and give a tribute to Dad. A daughter-in-law was the only volunteer. Linda, who has a heart bigger than Texas and wears it on her sleeve, also volunteered and asked that I come up to the podium to be with her and give her support. The evening prior to the funeral, she suggested that since I would be up there with her, perhaps I'd like to give a tribute to Dad myself. It's difficult to say no to her. She and I did not coordinate what to say, but it turned out well.

In *God Knew*, I shared with you the "love letter" I wrote to my mom and placed in her casket. If you will indulge me, I'd like to now share a portion of the tribute I gave for Dad at Discover Church in Oak Creek on November 8, 2022:

Dad's Tribute

Good evening. My name is Jim, and I belong to Linda.

What did Dad mean to me? It meant that I had an earthly father again for almost 5 years. God had called my biological dad home to heaven on August 7, 2012. I never thought I'd have a dad again. On our wedding day, Linda wrote me a letter. In that letter she mentioned how I now did have a dad again, and brothers and sisters in spades.

Dad and I never had any real in-depth talks about life. We didn't have any typical father/son discussions. What I did find out is that you shouldn't surprise him with things. As pastor mentioned, he was very contemplative. Some of you know this story and some of you don't but please allow me to share it again. When I knew things were getting serious between Linda and me, and I knew we were headed for marriage, I wanted to do things right. I'm an old-fashioned guy and Linda is an old-fashioned girl. I wanted to make sure I had Dad's approval and blessing before I asked Linda to marry me.

At that time, I would stay in their extra bedroom when I would visit Linda in Oak Creek. Dad was kind enough to allow that. So, one night, after Linda went to bed, I stood by the door of my bedroom and waited quietly for about 5 minutes. I slowly opened my bedroom door and peeked down the hallway. Linda's bedroom door was cracked open a bit in case Disney needed to get in. I heard the rain app going so I figured she was asleep. I quietly entered the hallway and made my way to the family room where Dad was still up, reading. He saw me and said, sort of loudly, "Hey Jim, what's up?" I went over to him, pulled up a chair, and said quietly, "I really love Linda, and she really loves me. She is the one for me and I'd like to ask her to marry me. But before I do, I want to be respectful to you and ask for your permission first. So, do I have your blessing to ask Linda to marry me?" He got a look on his face – not a bad look or a good look, but a look. After a little bit, he said, "I think so." Not exactly the enthusiastic response I was hoping for. I pressed on, "Because I wouldn't want to do anything you didn't approve of, and I won't ask her without your permission, so I'm wondering if I have your permission?" Again, the look...the pause...and the repeat of, "I think so." Okay... So, I said goodnight and went to my bed. As I lay there awake, I thought, "Well, he didn't say NO!"

A few weeks went by, and I was again in Oak Creek for the weekend. I arrived at his house on a Friday night, and I purposely left work early so I could beat Linda there. I pulled up a chair, had some general chit-chat with him, then I brought up the topic again. "A few weeks ago, I asked for your permission to ask Linda to marry me, and you said, 'I think so.' I just really want to make sure you are okay with this and that I have your blessing. Do I?" At that point, he had had time to think and digest what that really meant for him and for Linda and he said, "Yes, you do. She loves you and we all love you. I think you are great together. You have my blessing." Whew! I can't tell you what a relief that was since I already had a ring, Linda had purchased her dress, and we had the dates reserved at the churches. The remaining formality was the actual proposal, but that's a story for another time.

Linda and I haven't been physically worshipping at Discover Church for many months. If we would invite Dad to join us at worship on Sunday mornings, he would refuse. But, if we would watch worship online, he would watch with us. We felt that was a better use of our time.

On one of those Sundays, Linda was talking to Dad on the couch. She said how much she wanted to spend eternity in heaven with him. He said, "I know I'm not as demonstrative about my faith like you are, but I believe." But. I. Believe.

Dad would ask us to call him when we got home so he would know we arrived home safely. While Heaven doesn't have phones, Dad's declaration of faith, "But I believe," lets us know he arrived Home safely.

We did come to Discover Church this past weekend. Linda and I talked with Pastor Jon, who had visited Dad a few weeks ago. Linda was looking for reassurance from Jon as to Dad's faith. Jon gave us that reassurance, and then said words that will stick with me the rest of my life, "Linda, nobody loves your dad more than Jesus." I repeat, "nobody loves your dad more than Jesus."

And do you want to know something? Nobody loves YOU and me more than Jesus. He suffered and died for our sins and rose victorious over sin and death. That's real Love!

But your dad's love for all of you is a very close second. He loved each and every one of you and was so proud of his family. He loved to talk about his family.

Now, how many of you called Dad, or listened to him as he received a call, and heard him say in that low, mysterious voice, "Hello there!"? Sometimes it was just, "Hi, Honey" (that was to Linda, never to me) but usually his greeting was, "Hello there." It's tough to realize that we can't just pick up the phone and hear that greeting anymore, and wouldn't we all like to hear that again?

Follow me on something: last Wednesday night, around 7:15, God lovingly looked down, called him by the name given to him at his Baptism, and said "Dick, it's time." And as Dad passed through the gates of Heaven, there was Jesus, with a smile and a hug and a, "Welcome home! Well done, good & faithful servant." And as Dad looked over Jesus' shoulder, there was Fritzi (Linda's Mom), and Grandma Mell, and Keith (Linda's brother) and they looked at him, smiled, and said, "Hello there!"

And we know with certain hope, because we say with Dad, "But I believe," that someday God will call our name and say, "It's time." And we will pass through the gates of Heaven and Jesus will be there with a smile and a hug, and will say to us, "Welcome home! Well done, good & faithful servant!" And as we look over Jesus' shoulder, we will see Fritzi, Grandma Mell, Keith, and Dad standing there smiling. And we will hear Dad say once again "Hello there."

I miss both of my dads. Thankfully, by God's grace, both of them believed in Jesus as our Savior. So do I, and so does Linda. We wait with certain hope for that joyous reunion someday in heaven, where we will never be separated again. Ever.

CHAPTER 19
HE WHO PROMISED IS FAITHFUL

"He will wipe every tear from their eyes. There will be no more death'
or mourning or crying or pain, for the old order of things has passed
away." Revelation 21:4 (NIV)

I [Linda] would like to take the time to acknowledge and honor those who were not as blessed as our family was when it came to the pandemic and the loss of loved ones. I know that there were so many of you who have been to funeral after funeral and said more goodbyes than anyone could ever have imagined, or maybe you weren't even able to attend your loved one's funeral due to the C-word, and your hearts are blasted to pieces.

First, I want to tell you just how sorry I am that that happened to you. To think that you might not have had the opportunity to hug and kiss your mom, dad, grandma, grandpa, or God forbid, your child before they passed from this world breaks my heart. Second, it is my prayer that even through it all, you haven't lost your faith.

Having said that, maybe you haven't lost your faith, but maybe you have begun to doubt the goodness of God a little bit. And in those situations, it would be very hard for me to blame you. The enemy has gone full court press on this world, and he is doing every possible thing he can to kill, steal, and destroy. He would love nothing better than to cause you to turn your eyes away and turn your back on God. That's his sole reason for living.

But God. I truly believe that these things hurt God just as much as it hurts you. And, again, I know that it might be hard to believe that. He is God after all. But then I go back to the cross. I think of Jesus hanging there, carrying the weight of all our sins and the sins of every other person in the world for all time and God had to turn away from His own Son. But in allowing His one and only Son to die, the plan of salvation was accomplished. You and I can be with Him for eternity because of that plan.

Does hearing that help to heal the pain of your loss? Possibly not, but maybe it does bring you comfort. I would just ask you to not give up. Turn to Him and pour out your heart to Him. He promised in Revelation 21:4 (NIV) that, *"He will wipe every tear from their eyes. There will be no more death or mourning or crying or pain, for the old order of things has passed away."*

God sees you. He has seen your tears and He has heard your cries in the night. I beg you to let Him wrap you in His arms of love and to let the Holy Spirit comfort you.

For those of you who might not have gone through a loss like I mentioned above, but you are still waiting on God to answer your prayers, regardless of what they might be, I would just remind you to hold on to the promises in His Word. God has proven His goodness time and again to those who called out to Him. Here are just a few reminders in the Bible of God moving in seemingly impossible situations:

- Abraham was asked to sacrifice his only son, Isaac, but God stopped it just in time by providing a ram in Isaac's place.

- Isaac missed his mother Sarah, and God sent a servant to find a wife to comfort him.

- Moses and the Israelites were saved from Pharaoh when God opened the Red Sea for them to walk through on dry land.

- Hannah begged God for a son and God gave her a son.

- The Shunamite woman was barren, but because she honored the prophet, Elisha, God gave her the son she had despaired of ever having and then brought him back to life after he died of an unknown sickness after Elisha prayed.

- David cried out in distress after the loss of his son with Bathsheba, and God healed and restored his heart.

- Shadrach, Meshach, and Abednego believed God would protect them in the fiery furnace and Jesus met them there in the fire.

- Daniel believed God for protection in the lion's den and God closed the mouths of the lions and he walked out unharmed in the morning.

- The woman with the issue of blood let nothing hold her back from touching the hem of Jesus's garment. He healed her and called her "Daughter" and restored her back to health and wholeness.

- Peter having the ability to walk on the water to Jesus (as long as he kept his eyes on Jesus), and Jesus saving him from drowning when he looked at the waves.

- Jesus arising from the dead and showing Himself to His disciples after He took the sins of the world on His shoulders and saved humankind from eternal damnation.

These are just a few examples of God hearing the cries of His children and acting on their behalf. He loves you and hears your heart cries as well. He is always good, He is always just, and He is always faithful.

So, why did Jim and I sit down to write this book? Because we know with everything within us that we had a story to tell. Someone recently told us that our story is good, but it's not extraordinary. That stung a little bit at first. But, after thinking about it a bit, that person was right. Our story is a story about two rather ordinary people leading a rather ordinary life that just might give other ordinary people leading ordinary lives some hope. Another friend told us, "Not every story needs to be extraordinary. It's kind of nice to hear how God works in and through ordinary people. He does that a lot. It might just give them hope." We have a story of God's goodness and faithfulness that might just resonate with someone who has felt alone and possibly forgotten. A story for someone who has felt unloved. Someone who just needed to know that their struggles are not unique to them. Someone who needed to be reminded that protecting their virtue for marriage is an amazing thing and should be celebrated.

And maybe you just need to hear the words, "life is hard, but God is good." And as my friend Lysa TerKeurst says, "God is good; He is good to me, and He is good at being God." His ways are perfect, and His promises can be trusted, regardless of where you are in your life right now. He will sit with you in your pain and suffering. He is near to you in your loneliness and feelings of heartbreak.

He just wants to walk through this life with you. And if He chooses to give you the desires of your heart, praise Him. And if the answer is no or wait, praise Him. Because the goal is heaven and eternity with Him. If He blesses you here on earth with love and a family, be thankful and love them with your whole heart. But if He doesn't, search out friends who will draw you into their families and be Jesus with "skin on." Don't allow the ways of the world to draw you into their web but allow God to pour His love into you. Because He loves you and His love is unfailing.

As Psalm 91:1-2 and 14-16 (NLT) state, *"¹Those who live in the shelter of the Most High will find rest in the shadow of the Almighty. ²This I declare about the Lord: He alone is my refuge, my place of safety; he is my God, and I trust him." .... ¹⁴ The Lord says, "I will rescue those who love me. I will protect those who trust in my name. ¹⁵When they call on me, I will answer; I will be with them in trouble. I will rescue and honor them. ¹⁶I will reward them with a long life and give them my salvation."*

One of God's names is El Roi, the God who sees. Allow Him to hold you in your disappointment, in your disillusionment, and in your pain, and let Him be your all in all. Don't give up. Don't stop praying your *"but God You promised"* prayers. Surrender your will to Him and your heart to Him and He will show Himself faithful to you. Because that's another one of His names—Faithful and True—and His faithfulness is from everlasting to everlasting.

"Let us hold unswervingly to the hope we profess, for He who promised is faithful." Hebrews 10:23 (NIV)

CHAPTER 20
POTPOURRI

One of the challenges in co-authoring a book like this is that you both have a perspective on things, and you both want to tell the story, but some of the finer details might be missing. As I [Jim] mentioned in the Introduction, you may have already experienced some déjà vu when reading some of the same parts of a story over again, just from a slightly different angle.

This is a "potpourri" chapter; there is a little bit of this story, and a little bit of that story, with the intent of trying to fill in gaps where I think gaps exist. I couldn't think of a better way to do this, so you aren't left with too many lingering questions. So, here we go:

Our Faiths:

Yes, Linda and I are different faiths – I am a lifelong member of the Lutheran Church – Missouri Synod (LCMS), and Linda is a long-time member of the Assemblies of God (AG). You will notice from my "Impossible List" that the first "Must Have" is, "Christian (preferably LCMS or WELS Lutheran)." I knew from Linda's profile, and our first conversation, that she is strong in her faith, and she wasn't going to switch to LCMS for me. She knew I was strong in my faith, and I wasn't going to switch to AG for her. A few weeks later, after Linda and I had many phone conversations, I had lunch with Pastor Shoup to talk about this faith difference. He gave me some background into AG and told me that at the end of the day, they believe in Jesus as their Savior, which is the main thing that gave me comfort. There are differences in doctrines on almost everything else including the Lord's Supper, Baptism, Confession and Absolution, Rapture/End Times, Gifts of the Spirit, etc. As we mentioned, on Sundays we both attend Hope Community Church for Linda, and then St. Paul Lutheran in Bonduel for me. We both wanted to have a marriage where we worship together with our spouse, and we make it work. We worship together, we do Bible study together, and we pray together.

Our First Phone Call:

At the end of the "The Girl in the Red…Scarf?" chapter, I left you with the happy note that the girl in the red scarf wanted to talk. Linda told you a bit about that phone conversation. Here is my perspective:

I was incredibly nervous, and I don't really know why. I had gotten to the point of being numb and indifferent. I had gotten excited so many times, only to have that excitement shot down. But this time seemed different.

Linda and I talked for about 2 ½ hours that day. Yes, we found out we had a lot in common, an almost eerily amount in common. I had reached a point where I would just address the historic deal-breakers right from the start. I found that saves a lot of time. It was no different with Linda – I told her that many people wonder why I am 49 years old and still single. The reason was that I made the conscious decision to take care of my health-challenged, financially challenged parents, and I moved them in with me in 1998. I was following the Fourth Commandment to *"honor thy father and thy mother."* There was silence on the other end of the phone for several seconds. Linda then replied, "Jim, I took care of my mom, and now I'm looking after my dad, for the same reason." I thought, *"Wow! Here is a woman that understands what I went through."* When I found out she also likes Hallmark movies, I said, "I can't believe they haven't played my favorite Christmas movie yet, *Signed, Sealed, Delivered for Christmas.*" Again, a pause, and then, "Jim, you're not going to believe this, but that is my favorite Christmas movie, too!" The list of commonalities continued to grow.

The Discover Church Christmas Musical:

Other than going to downtown Milwaukee for the in-person interview for the professional matchmaking service, I couldn't tell you the last time I was in the Milwaukee area. I also couldn't tell you how many times my friends, Paul and Kristi Frisque, had invited me to come down for the weekend, and I never did.

As I drove down there that Friday afternoon to watch Linda in her church's musical that night, and to meet her for the first time afterward, I couldn't believe how long the drive was. I thought I would never get there. That didn't help my thought process regarding a long-distance relationship.

After unpacking at Paul and Kristi's (even though I refused their offers countless times, they were kind enough to open their home to me to stay that night), I ventured over to Discover Church. I had never been in an AG church that big before and it was overwhelming. I had a very warm, friendly greeting from Juan Carlos Hernandez, a wonderful man who is a long-time friend of Linda's, and now also a good friend of mine. I took my seat and was waiting for the show to begin.

Remember when I told you that my fear wasn't in the "no" anymore, but rather in the "yes?" Linda and I had talked several times. We scored insanely high on the eHarmony online compatibility test questions. She has a big heart, and I was deathly afraid I would disappoint her and break her heart at some point. She was just so "nice" and I didn't want to start something I wasn't sure I could finish. Plus, she was AG, and I was LCMS. She lived in Oak Creek and worked in Milwaukee, and I was living and working 2 ½ hours north. She had friends and family there, and I had friends and family here. How was this ever going to work? Maybe the best thing would be to just leave now, before the musical started, and send her a text that I wouldn't be pursuing this further.

But…my mom didn't raise me that way. I was (am) a gentleman. I am a Christian. I try to be a nice person and live by the Golden Rule. I strive for the Golden Result. And besides all of that, there was something inside of me that told me to keep my butt in that pew and not leave. That proverbial "gut feeling" told me that if I left and never looked back, I would deeply regret it for the rest of my life (talk about a What If? / If Only category!). I think that was a definite God knew moment. I will admit the urge to not meet Linda after the performance was also great, and yet there was some unseen Force leading me down the long corridor to the place where the actors were greeting the guests. Linda was dressed as the fishmonger she played in the musical, but there was a beauty that shone through the black soot on her face and the drabby costume she wore. At that point, we made plans to meet the next day for coffee. I had much less trepidation, and much more excitement, for that meeting. I thanked God that He kept me in that pew, in that church, and that I met the woman that would eventually, less than a year later, become my wife. God is always talking to us, but sometimes we just don't listen. Thankfully, His voice broke through all that clutter.

The Engagement:

Linda has already shared with you many details of our engagement – The Verragio, the Not-Verragio, the roses, the song, the dinner, etc., but I'm going to share with you a few "behind the scenes" things that went into that day. Single guys, a word of advice for you: if you really have found the "one" (you know she is the one because you have prayed and prayed about this, and she is "IT."), and you know you are going to propose only once in your life, then do it right and do it well. Make the extra effort and even spend the extra money (if you can) to make this a night your soon-to-be fiancé will never forget.

Number 1: don't mess with the ring like I did. We joke (sort of) about how Linda saw The Verragio and knew it was the perfect ring for her, and I looked at the price tag and decided we should look for a more affordable option. I know that Linda would have been very proud of The Not-Verragio ring and would have gladly shown it off. But, with The Verragio, THE ring, the way her eyes light up when she shows off her ring, or somebody compliments her on it, makes her relive all the happy memories of our engagement night and our wedding all over again. The extra couple hundred dollars is dwarfed by the happiness she shows.

Number 2: ask her dad for permission. Yes, I know it's old-fashioned and it's likely not done much anymore. In a prior chapter of this book, you read how that went for me initially – not as well as I had hoped. When you hope to get a resounding "yes, of course, you can marry my daughter" and you go to bed with the words, "I think so" echoing in your head, not once, but twice, it leaves you wondering. Thankfully, after Dad had time to think about it, he gave his blessing. It is a sign of respect. I know Dad appreciated it, and I am thankful that I did it. You will be, too.

Number 3: make it special. As Linda mentioned, we had been so busy introducing each other to family and friends, that we didn't have much "us" time. Coupled with the pressure I felt to "stop taking my sweet time" (that's from Linda's perspective, but she didn't know all the stuff I was lining up already to make this night extra special), I had to move quickly. We already had the dates, the dress, the ring, the proposed attendants, the honeymoon, etc. – we just needed the proposal. Here are some finer details:

1) The date. I chose a weekend when it was my turn to visit Linda. We already had plans on that Saturday night and Sunday, so Friday would have to be the date. But Fridays were casual dress days at Linda's employer, and I knew she wouldn't want engagement pictures in her jeans. Therefore, as she mentioned, I told her we would go on a "proper date" so she would bring a change of clothes.

2) The location. I asked several people, including Pastor Brooks, where the best location would be. He suggested Lake Park Bistro, so I checked it out online. It seemed like a nice place, so I booked a dinner reservation and let them know I'd be proposing. They wouldn't guarantee me a window seat, but I hoped we would get one.

I drove down early on Friday afternoon, dressed in a black suit with a blue dress shirt and a yellow tie (Linda's favorite color). That Friday was sunny, warm, and slightly humid. I set the air conditioning in my car to somewhere between "polar bear paradise" and "penguin delight," and, yet I was still sweating profusely because of my nerves. Engagement pictures in a sweat-soaked blue shirt would not have been attractive, so plan your wardrobe carefully.

Thankfully, I had brought along a white dress shirt. When I arrived at Lake Park Bistro, I met with the manager. I had brought a glass vase of flowers with white daisies (Linda's favorite) and six red roses that they would place on our table. I told the manager I was proposing, and had made a reservation, but they wouldn't guarantee me a window table. He told me not to worry – he would take care of us. He did.

I asked him where the best location would be to make the proposal. I had heard of a lighthouse and a bridge. He walked me over to the windows, pointed to a concrete landing, and said, "The bridge is under repair, the lighthouse is too far away, you should propose right there."

Then he asked me a question that I wasn't expecting, "How certain are you that she will say 'yes'?" I told him she had the dress, had picked out the ring, and we had the dates. He smiled and said, "Okay. So, you will propose before dinner and then I'll come out with some complimentary champagne, and then when you come back in, we will have your table by the window ready." I told him, "Um, I was planning on proposing after dinner. I have a photographer lined up to be here *after* dinner." He looked at me over his glasses and said, "You will propose before dinner." I wondered if I stuttered the first time, so I repeated myself, "No, I said after dinner." He smiled, put down his clipboard, and said, "I would highly recommend you propose before dinner. You are already nervous, and you don't want to be nervous throughout your dinner. If you propose before, and it sounds very certain she will accept, you will now come back in and have a celebratory dinner." Well, I thought that made sense, so I called the photographer, and he was able to come earlier. As it turned out, it started to rain when we were done with dinner, so it wouldn't have worked out if we had followed my plan. Be ready to adjust and adapt to the unexpected.

And, yes, I took the opportunity to change out of my sweat-soaked blue shirt and put on my clean white dress shirt. Plan to be nervous, and plan to sweat! I then went to pick up Linda from work.

3) Don't deceive and lie about your intentions on your "special date," but don't give it away, either. It took a lot to keep this plan a secret from Linda. While I kid her that I think she knew, I really do think I caught her by surprise. She didn't know some of the key things had already been taken care of

(i.e., asking her dad, asking Pastor Brooks, buying The Verragio, etc.). So, what seemed like a big, unnecessary delay on my part, was actually me getting everything lined up just right so I could exceed Linda's expectations. (I don't have to tell you (but I guess I will) that there is a parallel theme there with how God sometimes answers our prayers with, "Wait, I have something better planned.")

4) Hire a photographer. You will want to have some high-quality photos of this special occasion. Linda and I frequently look at those pictures and think about how good God is, and how grateful we are that He brought us together in such a special way.

Linda told you the story about me looking at my phone once we got to the landing area where I was going to propose. Here is the rest of that story – as I mentioned, because of the bistro manager's excellent suggestion, I had to coordinate the change with my photographer. As we reached the landing, my phone was exploding with a series of texts. Normally, I would have ignored them, but my fear was that it was Craig telling me he got caught up in traffic, or he wasn't in position, or his camera jammed. I didn't want to propose and not have pictures we could cherish. That is why I checked my phone. It turned out it was Craig; however, he was letting me know he was there, he was set up, and I could propose at any time.

Then, Linda turned around. I was afraid she would see Craig, recognize her friend was there, and figure it all out. Thankfully, Craig had on a baseball cap, and his camera was up at his face, so Linda thought it was regular paparazzi. Whew! God even had that small detail covered.

5) Celebrate!! No, don't get "fall off your barstool" drunk. Next to your wedding day, this will be the most momentous day in your relationship (unless, of course, God blesses you with children). Savor it, remember it, and celebrate it! You would

be surprised how quickly the time goes. As Linda mentioned, we immediately got on social media and texted our close friends and family so everybody could help us celebrate the long-awaited answer to many prayers. This leads me to that last one...

6) Pray. I saved the best piece of advice for last, but it should be the first thing you do. Hopefully, while you have been dating and getting to know each other, you have been praying together about your relationship and asking God to lead and guide you. Now, on the day you are going to propose, pray even harder. Then, be still, and listen to God. Even though I had all the details worked out, I prayed and asked God one final time if this was His will for me, and us. It was, and it is.

Now, if money is tight, you can still make it extra special. Pick a nice, but not expensive restaurant. Buy the best ring you can afford. One rose will be as special as a bouquet. Have a friend show up and take some pictures. You can still do this right, and do this well, without breaking the bank.

CHAPTER 21
WHAT IF? / IF ONLY

In *God Knew*, I shared with you my favorite game – the game of "What If?" and its counterpart, "If Only." I warned you I was an expert at that game, and I even proved it to you by giving example after example of how well I played that potentially deadly game.

I just wanted to circle back on that to let you know that I don't play that game anymore. Oh yes, there are days the devil tries to get in my head and tempt me to start playing. Thankfully, I know the secret now to winning that game. And you could say that God knew that secret all along.

There it is – the secret. *God knew* is the secret.

Allow me to explain. Every once in a while, I have a really bad day (well, "bad" is a relative term; I should say "bad for Jim" sort of day. Many people would trade for my bad days). Nothing seems to be going right and I start to question myself and my abilities. Nobody and nothing seem to help. That's when the devil tries to get me to play:

- What if I had taken a different job?
- If only things had worked out for us to move away.
- What if I had gone to school for a different career path?
- If only that person wasn't such an insufferable jerk.

Then, for good measure, the devil starts to get very personal again:

- Jim, you know you could have been there when your mom died. If only you hadn't slept in a little longer. What if your mom needed you as she was dying – you weren't there!

- Jim, there were times you didn't treat your dad very well. If only you could take all those times back. You weren't always a very good son!

- Jim, remember those times when your mom wanted to play cards, go for a drive, or just talk to you, but you brushed her off? How do think that made her feel? How disrespectful? What if you had not been so selfish? Think of all the additional great memories you would have!

- Jim, Dr. Gillis told you that dialysis would likely pro-long your mom's life. She might still be here today if you had made a different medical decision. If only your mom could have been here to meet Linda, to see you two get married, and to be a part of your life together now!

I know it sounds like I really *do* still play that game. There is a lot of guilt still housed in those What If / If Only statements.

Allow me to share with you what happens when I start to get tempted. Let's take the first personal attack for example: the devil tries to make me feel guilty for not being there when my mom died. When that starts to happen, I remember the words of CNA, Pam, "Jim, if God thinks you're strong enough to be there when your mom dies, you will be. If He doesn't, you won't be." When the devil still persists with the haunting and accusatory words, "You. Weren't. There!" I just look back at him and reply, "You know what, you're right. I wasn't there when my mom breathed her last. God knew I wasn't strong enough to watch my beautiful, loving mother take her last breath. God knew Mom didn't want me to endure that sight, so she gave up when she knew I wasn't there. No, devil, I wasn't there. But Jesus was! I couldn't take Mom's hand and walk her through the valley of the shadow of death and into Heaven, but Jesus could. I couldn't welcome her into her eternal Home she always longed for, but Jesus could. My human hands could have done nothing special to save my mom at that time, but Jesus' nail-pierced hands had already done everything to save my mom. Whether or not I was there when my mom died was relatively inconsequential. Jesus being there when Mom died was literally a matter of eternal life or eternal death. She was in the best hands possible when she died. The One that really mattered *was* there."

Or how about the second example: the times I didn't treat my dad very well. My earthly father experienced all those times, and my heavenly Father saw all those times. A father's love is a beautiful and wonderful thing; our heavenly Father's love is an amazing and incomprehensible thing. God knew I couldn't live with that earthly unforgiven guilt for the rest of my life. God knew there was a way for forgiveness to happen. So, He gave us an advanced warning of my dad's death. And during that time, I took advantage of that opportunity. I confessed those sins to my father. At first, I thought it was perhaps his Alzheimer's Disease that was causing him to not remember those sins anymore. Then I realized, Dad had just chosen to forgive them and forget them when they happened. I was dredging up sins my dad wasn't even holding against me anymore. I also confessed those sins to God and asked Him for forgiveness. Jesus tapped me on the shoulder with His nail-pierced hand, pointed to the cross, and said, "Jim, it appears you've forgotten that I already took care of all those sins on the cross. I already paid the full price for them. You are forgiven! Let them go!" My heavenly Father then reminds me of His promise in Jeremiah 31:34 (ESV), *"...For I will forgive their iniquity, and I will remember their sin no more."* My earthly father followed the example of my heavenly Father – he remembered my sin no more. And he did that because of his love for his son, and also his love for the Son. God forgives me because of his love for his son, and also His love for His only begotten Son, who takes away the sin of the world! God knew we needed a Savior, so He sent Jesus.

With those quick God knew responses when the devil starts to tempt me with guilt, it shuts those games down fast.

Now, let me share with you the way this game typically plays out now, and how it causes me to marvel at God's love and faithfulness, and highlights the fact that God knew:

- What if I hadn't emailed Linda on eHarmony when I realized they had matched us a year earlier, and that she lived two and a half hours away? I could've. But God knew.

- What if, when I went down to Oak Creek that first time to meet Linda, I had followed the temptation to just get up and leave the performance, and not meet this wonderful woman of God? I would've. But God knew.

- What if, when Linda and I were having continuing arguments about a contentious issue while we were dating, and it didn't appear we could reach a resolution, I had just called things off? Circumstances said likely I should've. But God knew. (By the way, that issue did get resolved – again, God knew).

Ah, "could've, would've, should've." Someone has called those three contractions the "holy trinity of regret." Well, my regret would be real if I had followed any one of those temptations. God knew exactly the woman He had for me, and He made sure we met, and that my insecurities and overthinking didn't get in the way. As you've read, Linda and I have an amazing life, and an amazing God knew love story – a story He wrote long ago.

Let's face it, temptations do come, every day. Regrets also come every day. There will always be What If / If Only scenarios that distract us. But there is no positive outcome if you let them eat you up and take over your mind and your heart. Instead of letting the holy trinity of regret run, and ruin, your life, let the Holy Trinity, Father, Son, and Holy Spirit, rule your hearts and minds. As we read in Colossians 3:15a (ESV), *"And let the peace of Christ rule in your hearts."* Also, in Philippians 4:7 (ESV), *"And the peace of God, which surpasses all understanding, will guard your hearts and your minds in Christ Jesus."*

When you put your faith in Jesus as your Lord and Savior, you will have no eternal regrets. My mom and dad knew that, and they are now in God's nearer presence, waiting for the day when Jesus comes back again and takes all believers to heaven. The Holy Spirit is with us right now, giving us the faith to believe in Jesus. He nourishes, sustains, and strengthens that faith through God's Word and the Sacraments. God is always with us, always watching out for us, protecting us from evil and disasters we don't even know about. Sometimes bad things do happen in our sinful world. But we know and rest in the confidence that God is in control. He has already defeated sin, death, and the power of the devil. The empty cross, and the empty tomb, are proof of that.

CHAPTER 22
FAITHFULNESS FULFILLED

"Know therefore that the LORD your God is God; he is the faithful God, keeping his covenant of love to a thousand generations of those who love him and keep his commandments." Deuteronomy 7:9 (NIV)

"God is good, all the time! And all the time, God is good!" We hear those words so often, and sometimes they become a catchy phrase that we say and repeat, but do we always believe it? Can I [Linda] say that I always did 100% of the time? No, honestly, I will admit that there were times when I wasn't sure where God was and why my dreams didn't always come true, and my prayers seemingly weren't answered. But God knew.

And over this life-long journey of mine with God, I have come to a place where I can say "It is well with my soul." Because through this journey, I was not only able to say that I found in Jim the "one who my soul loves" but I have found in God, the "One who loves my soul." And the One who loves my soul is good, He is kind, He is Love. And, I can say, wholeheartedly that His faithfulness has been fulfilled in my life. I am ever grateful; I am ever humbled, and I am ever His.

And now we have come to the end of my story...well, hopefully, just in this book. I hope and pray to have many more years to love, serve, and do life with my amazing husband. To prayerfully be used as God's servant to do just what my friend Nicki said in my earlier chapter and help to impact generations of women who need to hear of the hope of God's love and to encourage them to allow God to use them, too. Just know that Jim and I love you and we are praying that God will be as faithful to you as He has been to us.

CHAPTER 23
"I HAD IT ALL THE WAY"

[16]"But to what shall I compare this generation? It is like children sitting in the marketplaces and calling to their playmates, [17]'We played the flute for you, and you did not dance; we sang a dirge, and you did not mourn.'" Matthew 11:16-17 (ESV)

There is a great Christian movie from 2019 called, *Play the Flute*. When Linda first suggested we watch this movie for our regular Friday night date-night, I balked. Ugh – who wants to watch a movie that would seem to be about a talented musical specialist in an orchestra, right? Wrong! This is such a great Christian movie that I would encourage you to watch it. We ended up watching it three times.

The synopsis from IMDB states, "Faced with an indifferent youth group, a new youth Pastor (Brett Varvel) tries to motivate his students to read God's Word and get serious about their faith." There are many, many good life and faith lessons in this movie.

One of the lessons is a story the pastor tells about an airline flight that was especially scary. He said he had never been on a flight like this before, with all the turbulence and uncertainty, and just how scared he was. The fear among the passengers was so real, and he prayed very hard. Ultimately, the plane landed safely. He said that while it was customary for the flight attendants to greet the passengers as they were getting off the plane, the captain himself was performing that duty. As he greeted the pilot, he told him of the fear he experienced. The pilot, with a very calm and reassuring voice, said, "There was no need to be scared. I had it all the way." The pastor admits that he couldn't fly that airplane – all he could do was trust the pilot. He had to trust that the pilot had it all the way.

He continued the lesson with the youth by stating how death can be a scary thing. For those of us who have followed Jesus, we are going to have to trust that Jesus had it all the way. We have to trust that

Jesus will do what He said He would do, and usher us into the presence of God.

As Linda and I were talking after watching the movie, I told her I wanted to use this story from that movie in this book. She agreed that was a good idea. Then, it dawned on me – "I had it all the way" is God's perspective on the things we view as "God Knew" moments.

Allow me to recap a few of our real-life examples:

- *Death* – my dad died in 2012; my mom died in 2014. I thought my life had ended. I had no purpose in life, no wife, no girlfriend. I was alone. Totally and completely alone. I was so scared the grief would never end; I was so scared the loneliness would never end. Then I think about all the things God has orchestrated in my life since my parents passed, how He has guided me and led me along the way, and how He walked with me, upheld me, and comforted me. I look at the ways He did that and say, "God Knew." God smiles and says, "There was no need to be scared, Jim. I had it all the way."

- *My job* – in 2016, I didn't know what I was going to do. I felt trapped, anxious, and hopeless, stuck in a job that was literally sucking the life out of me. I was scared for my future. I look at the resolution as God Knew; God just lovingly smiled and said, "There was no need to be scared, Jim. I had it all the way."

- *My love life* – up until 2017, I thought I had tried everything imaginable to find a wife to share my life with. Online dating, friends, family, professional matchmaking, grocery stores (yes, that's a real thing), etc. I had dates, but nothing panned out. Were my expectations too high? Perhaps. Was I tempted to lower them to escape the intense loneliness? Yes. Did I cave? No. Facing an uncertain and perhaps very ominous future alone can be a very scary scenario. You read about Linda and how we met, and how we are living our happily ever after here on earth. We look at God bringing us together as God Knew; God looked at us and said, "Jim and Linda, there was no need to be scared. I had it all the way."

- *Linda's job* – when she moved up here, she interviewed at many places in Shawano, Green Bay, and DePere. As those opportunities faded away one by one, anxiety and fear set in. When I came home from work that Monday in December to find Linda crying because the last job opportunity was gone and we had a deadline to purchase a new home we weren't going to meet, she tearfully questioned, "What are we going to do?" God was right there next to us, reassuring us, "Jim and Linda, there is no need to be scared. I have it all the way." And He did. He provided Linda with a great job, working from our remodeled home in Shawano.

- *Our new home purchase* – we loved that house. We wanted that house. It would be a great way to start our new lives together in *our* new home. It was God's guidance that caused us to put in the financing contingency that Linda had to find a job by 12/31 or we could cancel. She didn't, so we did. And we are absolutely loving our remodeled home with a mortgage of less than half of what we would have had. At that time, we saw an uncertain housing future. God smiled and said, "Don't be scared. I have it all the way."

- *Linda's entire life story* – the same struggles, fears, heartaches, doubts, and uncertainty I experienced. God smiled at her and said, "Linda, there is no need to be scared. I had it all the way."

Do you remember the story about Jesus calming the storm? The Gospels of Matthew, Mark, and Luke all record this amazing event. Here is how it is told in Mark 4:35-41 (ESV):

> *35 On that day, when evening had come, he said to them, "Let us go across to the other side." 36 And leaving the crowd, they took him with them in the boat, just as he was. And other boats were with him. 37 And a great windstorm arose, and the waves were breaking into the*

boat, so that the boat was already filling. ³⁸ But he was in the stern, asleep on the cushion. And they woke him and said to him, "Teacher, do you not care that we are perishing?" ³⁹ And he awoke and rebuked the wind and said to the sea, "Peace! Be still!" And the wind ceased, and there was a great calm. ⁴⁰ He said to them, "Why are you so afraid? Have you still no faith?" ⁴¹ And they were filled with great fear and said to one another, "Who then is this, that even the wind and the sea obey him?"

Look again at Mark 4:40. We could paraphrase Jesus' words, "There was no need to be afraid. I had it all the way."

Or how about the story of Jesus raising Lazarus from the dead, as recorded in John 11:17-37 (ESV), with special emphasis on these verses 32-36 and 38-40:

³² Now when Mary came to where Jesus was and saw him, she fell at his feet, saying to him, "Lord, if you had been here, my brother would not have died." ³³ When Jesus saw her weeping, and the Jews who had come with her also weeping, he was deeply moved in his spirit and greatly troubled. ³⁴ And he said, "Where have you laid him?" They said to him, "Lord, come and see." ³⁵ Jesus wept.

³⁸ Then Jesus, deeply moved again, came to the tomb. It was a cave, and a stone lay against it. ³⁹ Jesus said, "Take away the stone." Martha, the sister of the dead man, said to him, "Lord, by this time there will be an odor, for he has been dead four days." ⁴⁰ Jesus said to her, "Did I not tell you that if you believed you would see the glory of God?"

An all too human Jesus grieves at the death of His friend Lazarus. This same Jesus knew how things were going to turn out in a few minutes. Death was not a part of God's original plan for His creation. Just because you know things will ultimately turn out alright doesn't mean you can't cry when sad things happen. While Lazarus's sisters grieved their brother and were likely confused as to why Jesus didn't come and save him, they ultimately got the message from Jesus, "There was no need to be afraid. I had it all the way."

One more example: the thief on the cross. His deathbed (or in this case, death-cross) confession is recorded in Luke 23:39-43 (ESV),

> *"39 One of the criminals who were hanged railed at him,[a] saying, "Are you not the Christ? Save yourself and us!" 40 But the other rebuked him, saying, "Do you not fear God, since you are under the same sentence of condemnation? 41 And we indeed justly, for we are receiving the due reward of our deeds; but this man has done nothing wrong." 42 And he said, "Jesus, remember me when you come into your kingdom." 43 And he said to him, "Truly, I say to you, today you will be with me in paradise."*

We don't know much about that man on the cross next to Jesus, but we do know he was a criminal that committed a crime punishable by death, and that he was given the faith to recognize Jesus as the Messiah. His plea for mercy was met with, "There is no need to be afraid. I have it all the way." And Jesus can respond to the criminal with such confidence because He knows His Father has it all the way. The plan of salvation is nearing completion. "It is finished" will soon reverberate through the air. And three days later, the empty tomb will put the exclamation mark on "I had it all the way!"

How about your life? Can you look back now and recognize the "God Knew" moments – those moments when you had no idea what was happening or why, and now you do? Can you picture God coming to you in those moments, maybe through the reassurances of reading His Word, the family or friends He has placed in your life, or a beloved pastor, and saying, "My child, there is no need to be afraid. I had it all the way!"

One day, at a time only known to the Father, Jesus will come again. He will wipe away all tears, all pain, all suffering, all sin, all death, Satan – everything bad. For those who believe in Him, He will take them by the hand, usher them through the valley of the shadow of death, and into an eternal paradise. He has proven time and time again that He is faithful and that we can trust Him. There truly is no need for us to be afraid; we can be confident that Jesus has it (and us) all the way!

CHAPTER 24
I CAN'T CHANGE THE TERMS

Congratulations! Once again, you've made it to the next-to-last chapter of a *God Knew* book! Linda and I are very grateful for you.

Please allow me to share one more story from *Play the Flute* that fits into our theme of faithfulness fulfilled: the lead character, a youth pastor named Brandon, is trying to return a blouse his wife purchased from a local store. He has the blouse, and the receipt. Should be an easy transaction, right? The cashier looks at both, smiles, and calmly replies that the blouse cannot be returned because it was on the "All Sales Final" rack. Even a little bit of pleading by the pastor doesn't do any good. The cashier finally smiles an even bigger, genuine smile and says, "I'm sorry, sir. Those were the terms of the sale, and I can't change the terms."

Has this scenario ever happened to you? You bought something and it wasn't what you expected, or it was broken, or it didn't fit. You thought, "Hey, I have the receipt. I have proof I purchased this. I'll just take it back, return it, and get my money back." Then when you get to the store, they tell you they're terribly sorry, but they can't take the item back, and they won't give you the money back. The sale ends up being final, and you are left disappointed, discouraged, and dissatisfied. Sometimes, it's the "fine print" that gets us.

The pastor in the movie used his experience to demonstrate to his youth group an important Biblical truth we all need to understand clearly: I can't change the terms. You can't change the terms.

You might be asking: what terms are those? God's terms for salvation.

As I was thinking about this chapter, it occurred to me that one of the first terms recorded in the Bible is in Genesis 2:16 (ESV, emphasis mine), *"And the Lord God commanded the man, saying, "You may surely eat of every tree of the garden, but of the tree of the knowledge of* *good and evil you shall not eat, <u>for in the day that you eat of it you shall surely die.</u>"* Those seem to be some pretty clear terms; terms for which there are no returns.

We know what happened – the serpent tempted Eve, Eve ate, Adam ate, and sin entered the world. They bought the lies the devil was selling, and there were no returns. They had eaten from the "All Sales Final" tree, and that tree extracts a heavy price. Per God's command, the death sentence was delivered.

What is God's reaction to this disobedience? His terms were clear (disobedience = death), and the terms were violated. Did He command Adam and Eve to do something in an attempt to make things right again? They couldn't. Did He want to return His damaged creation? He couldn't – He created them; they were already His. No, He couldn't return them, but He could redeem them. There was nothing Adam and Eve could do, but God knew there was something *He* could do. In Genesis 3:15 (ESV, bold mine), God says, "*I will*..." God knew He was the only One who could come up with a plan to redeem His creation. God always sets the terms, and, because He is faithful, He abides by those terms. Adam and Eve must physically die, but with the promise of a Savior, they wouldn't have to spiritually die.

The world might tempt us to think: Whew! *Adam and Eve* disobeyed, and *Adam and Eve* must die. We can fool ourselves into thinking we might be off the hook on this.

Allow me to share some other biblical terms with you (all ESV, emphasis mine):

- *"for **all** have sinned and fall short of the glory of God."* – Romans 3:23
- *"Therefore, just as sin came into the world through one man, and death through sin, and so death spread to **all** men because **all sinned**..."* – Romans 5:12
- And the final judgment words, *"For the wages of sin **is** death."* – Romans 6:23

"Is" is such a definite term, isn't it? Romans 6:23 doesn't say, "For the wages of sin could be/might be death." It says it "is" death.

Death. Death is a horrible thing to think about. It makes me think of sadness, helplessness, and mourning.

The verse from Matthew 11:17 ends with the words, *"and you did not mourn."* Nobody likes to mourn. If we are mourning, it means we have lost something or someone, we loved very much. Sometimes, the emotional hurt is so deep that it becomes physical hurt. Nobody chooses to mourn. Nobody chooses to hurt. Nobody chooses to be separated from the one they love the most. As you read in the original *God Knew*, in this sequel, and in my blog posts after my mom died, I was mourning. I still am. I didn't choose to have my mom die. I didn't choose that hurt. I didn't choose to be separated from the one I loved the most. I was confused, bewildered, mourning, and wondering what was going to happen next. And I will continue to mourn for my mom until she and I are reunited in Heaven someday with our Savior, my dad, and all those who have gone before us in the faith.

On Good Friday, there was mourning. Jesus' mother and His disciple John were there, mourning. There were others there, too, con-fused, bewildered, mourning, and wondering what was going to happen next.

But God knew.

God knew His plan of salvation was being fulfilled. God knew that He was showing the world His faithfulness to fulfill His promise of a Savior that He made in the Garden of Eden. The *"I will..."* of Genesis 3:15 became "I did" the night Jesus was born.

God knew a few other things, too:

- You were going to be born, and not only be born, but be born in sin

- Just like Adam and Eve, you could do nothing, and I mean nothing, on your own to repair your broken relationship with God

- The only way to repair the broken relationship with God because of sin was to have a sacrifice so big, so perfect, it would have to be God Himself

- Jesus, God's only begotten Son, would be the only One capable of being that Sacrifice

As Jesus hung on that cross, taking the punishment for your sins and mine, He thought of you, and He thought of me. He knew what had to be done. He knew the price it would cost Him to make sure you would be forever in heaven with Him. That price was His very life. We read in 1 Corinthians 6:20a (ESV), *"...for you were bought with a price."*

From all eternity past, Jesus had never been separated from His Father, and yet, He chose the pain. He chose the nails. He chose the separation from the One He loves the most so He could spend eternity with the ones He loves the most. John 15:13 (ESV) says, *"Greater love has no one than this, that someone lay down his life for his friends."* And then the beautiful words of John 3:16 (KJV) remind us, *"For God so loved the world that He gave His only begotten Son, that whosoever believes in Him shall not perish, but have everlasting life."*

These are the terms, God's terms, as written in Mark 16:16 (ESV), *"Whoever believes and is baptized will be saved, but whoever does not believe will be condemned."* You and I can't change the terms.

The blood of Jesus paid the price, in full, for all our sins. His blood bought our freedom – once and for all, for all who believe in Him. The devil may try to bargain with you to convince you that you are still his. He will bring up certain sins, secret sins, to make you believe that maybe, just maybe, the cross wasn't enough. But there stands Jesus, with His nail-pierced hands, looking the devil squarely in the eye and declaring, "This one is mine. I paid the price for every single one of his/her sins. All sales are final. You can't change the terms."

How can we be assured the "sale" was final? Jesus declared it so when He cried out, "It is finished!" God's plan of salvation was finished, complete, and final. No returns. No exceptions.

Sometimes, all we can do is play the flute – share our faith with others, and the reason for our hope (2 Peter 2:15). In this book, Linda and I hope we have played the flute, to the best of our ability, with a tune that is based entirely on God's Word. We are not perfect. We make mistakes. And guess what? So does the person reading this book. We are not judging anybody – we are simply reminding you what God's Word says…we are reminding you of the terms. We share God's terms out of love. We do not think we are better than anybody else – we are all sinners and beggars before the throne of God asking for forgiveness.

Forgiveness. That is also something sorely lacking in society today. Nobody wants to take responsibility for their actions and their errors. It's easier to pass the buck than to admit you were wrong. It's easier to try to manipulate the terms to match your sin and make it "okay." And as society continues to warp and pervert what is right and wrong, it's easier and easier to think you don't need forgiveness. If you don't need forgiveness, then there is no need for a Savior, right?

But God's Word is very clear that we do need forgiveness, and therefore we do need a Savior because there is nothing we can do on our own to restore our relationship with God. God knew that even before the fall into sin, so He sent His only begotten Son, Jesus, into this world, to live a perfect life, take all of our sins upon Himself on the cross to pay their penalty, die the death meant for us, and to rise again three days later to defeat sin, death, and the devil.

There is another problem in society today: context. People take little bits and pieces and snippets and sound bites and twist the words to fit their agenda…and to create doubt. Satan did that in the Garden with, "Did God really say?" Satan tries to do that today, too. Take Romans 6:23 (NIV) above, *"For the wages of sin is death."* The terms are clear: sin = death. If that is where God's Word ended, we would, indeed, be doomed. Thank God that passage continues, not with fine print, but with a fine promise, "For the wages of sin is death, *but the free gift of God is eternal life in Christ Jesus our Lord."* How would God redeem His creation? With the free gift of His Son, our Redeemer, Jesus Christ.

Those are the terms. I can't change them. You can't change them. And I wouldn't want them changed. You and I were bought with a price. All sales final means that you and I will be with God forever in heaven.

Heaven. The ultimate "Happily Ever After" destination for Christians. Everyone who believes the terms of salvation will be there. I will be, and so will Linda. We know our parents and other loved ones are there, in God's nearer presence, waiting for a joyous reunion. They are already enjoying their "happily ever after."

Until that day, Linda and I will live out our lives playing the flute, proclaiming God's grace and mercy, fulfilling the Great Commission to tell all nations about the Gospel, and reminding everyone that no matter what you are going through, God is always right by your side, He has it all the way, and that, God knew! We know that whether it is in this life, or the life to come, you can rest assured: they (you) lived happily ever after.

Until next time. God bless!

Your friends,
Jim & Linda

CHAPTER 25
THE FUTURE OF GOD KNEW

The Future of God Knew:

There is one important thing that falls into the timeline of my singleness, and it happened right before I met Linda – a vision for a *God Knew* ministry.

I released the original *God Knew* in April 2015. I sold a fair amount of softcover books myself at local book signings. My online sales were okay but not stellar. I had invested in several book marketing strategies with limited success. In November 2017, literally two weeks before I met Linda on eHarmony, I flew out to Philadelphia for a book marketing conference, and I took my good friend, Greg, along. During that conference, I came up with a vision for a series of *God Knew* books, Bible studies, podcasts, merchandise, etc. A dream was born. I came up with an actual vision board for this dream. When I showed it to Linda, she told me about the story she shared with you about her friend, Nicki's message to her. Linda is all-in on this vision.

Linda and I believe the time is right to get things in motion. God is opening doors and putting very special people in our lives to help us in this endeavor. This second book is the first step. We have a brand-new website and some merchandise. At the end of this chapter, you can find out how you could potentially be part of a future *God Knew* book.

Linda and I ask for your prayers and that God's will is done through us. To Him alone be the glory!

<u>Your "God Knew" Story</u>

Since *God Knew* was first released in 2015, I have had countless people come up to me and share their own "God knew" story. It is always heartwarming to hear how God is working in the lives of regular, everyday ordinary people. He cares about every one of us so much!

Do you want to potentially be part of a future *God Knew* book? If you have your own *God Knew* story (and we're sure you do), and you'd like to share it for consideration for an upcoming *God Knew* book, please visit our website at www.Godknew.org, and click on the "Submit A Story" page. If your story conforms to the beliefs in the Introduction, and to the requirements on our webpage, we will consider including your story in a future compilation book.

Thank you for reading this book. We pray you have been blessed by it!

EPILOGUE
THEY LIVED HAPPILY EVER AFTER

Writing is a funny thing – you think you're done and then another thought strikes you.

At the opening of this book, I wrote about the "Five Life-Changing Words" everybody likes to hear, "they lived happily ever after." In a prior chapter, I wrote about how we can get to that happily ever after, in this life, and the next. We get to it through God's unchanging terms.

You also have finished reading what I promised you was an almost unbelievable love story. I think you will agree that Linda and me being together is no mere coincidence – it is a "God-cidence" of epic proportions. Only God could have written our love story and made it come to life. You have now met my beautiful wife, Linda. You know her story, and how her story parallels my own in so many ways until God caused the parallel lines of this "Momma's Boy" and that "Daddy's Girl" to intersect at just the right place and time. You also know that God knew.

If you've been married for even a short period of time, you will relate to what I'm about to say. If you've never been married, I'm sorry to squash any illusions you may have about your future happily ever after life. Here is what "happily ever after" looks like:

- It's job stress that spills over into your quality time together
- It's in-laws and friends that can cause strife
- It's headaches, tummy aches, doctor visits, chiropractor visits, and specialists
- It's being too busy and tired to cook so you run through a drive-thru
- It's getting lost in social media during your evening together because you just need to get away from reality
- It's disagreements about little, inconsequential things
- It's disagreements about big things

- It's burps and gas and bad breath
- It's figuring out how to pay bills when the money just isn't there
- It's, "I'm sorry, not tonight, honey"
- It's holding your tongue, taking a deep breath, and counting to 10, sometimes multiple times in the day, while rolling your eyes (Pro-tip: keep them closed)

Perhaps you just looked back up to the top of the list to see if I really said *happily* ever after?

When I was a kid growing up, there was a TV show called "The Facts of Life," with a theme song by the same name. There is a line from that song that goes, "You take the good, you take the bad, you take them both and there you have the facts of life."

That previous list emphasized the "bad." Now, here are the good "facts of life":

- It's coming home after a long day to your fortress of solitude. I'm not talking about a building when I say fortress – I'm talking about your spouse – your fortress who is your safe place to decompress and unload.
- It's knowing that even though you may fight at times, your spouse will fight anybody else twice as hard for you.
- It's knowing that you have somebody you can be real with.
- It's knowing that life happens, and you are a team – the same team. The two became one on your wedding day.
- It's knowing it's okay to not win every fight. Compromise is not a bad thing. Linda and I differ on how best to load the dishwasher. Is that really a hill I'm willing to die on, or risk my marriage over? No way.

Best of all, it's knowing that Linda and I aren't doing this alone. As you've read numerous times, the key to a successful marriage comes down to the Third Person in your marriage – Jesus. How is He integrated into our marriage?

- Linda and I pray together before every meal
- We listen to Christian music instead of secular music
- We attend worship together, even though we belong to different denominations. We respect each other's beliefs, and we learn. We are both Christians, we both believe in Jesus as our only Savior, and we are both going to heaven someday
- We ask God to be a part of every discussion and every decision we make
- When we have intense discussions where we do/may disagree, we pray before and we hold hands during our talk. It helps us to remember we are on the same team; one team
- We pray that everything we say and do will bring glory to God
- We pray every night that He will continue to be the Third and most important Strand in our marriage and that He will continue to bless, guard, protect, defend, and strengthen our marriage
- We pray together, out loud, before bed
- We pray, separately, when we get up (we get up at different times)
- We pray before every trip that God will be with us and protect us

And when we pray, we know our prayers don't have far to go. Jesus is right there with us – when we eat, when we travel, when we go to bed, and when we get up. He is simply and always there. He is here right now with me in our dining room as I type these words. He is also with Linda right now as she is in the family room typing her story. He is with thousands, even millions, of people, right now at this same time, watching over them, protecting them, and listening to them. We do have, and serve, a truly great God.

Linda was born in 1970; I was born in 1968. Our lives began that day. We were born again into God's family through the waters of Holy

Baptism. And we both had new lives starting on November 26, 2017. We will live our happily ever after in this life, just me and Linda and Jesus, until He decides it's time for us to go Home, and this earthly life ends. That is when our true happily ever after begins – and our perfect sanctified life begins – an eternal chapter that will never end.

ABOUT THE AUTHORS

Jim Meyer was born and raised in Northeast Wisconsin, the only child of Ralph and Lorraine Meyer. Meyer has always loved to touch lives through the written word. In 2015, he published the first book in the God Knew series, Revelations of God's Grace in Unexpected Ways. His devotions have also been featured in Portals of Prayer. A banker by trade and a child of God with his Shepherd's heart, Meyer is in the world, but not of it. His writing is real, authentic, and transparent. In 2018, he married the love of his life, Linda – the long-awaited answer to many prayers. They reside in Shawano and enjoy spending time with family and friends.

Linda Meyer was born and raised in Oak Creek, Wisconsin, and is one of 7 children in her family. Linda has a strong Christian faith, loves God, and wants to serve Him by using her gifts of writing to share the hope of Christ with those needing encouragement. She was very involved in the music and women's ministries at the home church she attended for 32 years.

Linda also volunteered with the Online Bible Studies arm of Proverbs 31 Ministries for several years. After she met and married Jim, she moved from her hometown "up north" to the quaint little town of Shawano, Wisconsin. She and Jim love to cook and enjoy opening their home to friends and family for fun and fellowship and a fire on their patio. Just two normal people who want to share the love of Jesus and provide hope to a hurting world.